Your Magnificent Self...

A Journey to Freedom

'*Consciousness expands and Humankind takes a quantum leap into the unknown as they discover how to go beyond seduction, limitation, the ailing and ageing body and the death trigger. They enjoy living and creating as Loving DivineHumanBeings in a time-less space of freedom and an expanding field of potential where they experience rejuvenation, abundance and an infinite flow of pure love and joy.*'

'*My story is a magnificent LOVE story between my Divine and Human selves... who find each other after many years apart and become ONE. It is an amazing journey of exploration, expanding my consciousness, my awareness and my mind becoming quiet. In this quietness I AM able to observe and feel the integration that is naturally taking place and become... A Loving and Magnificent Master Creator who chooses, expresses and creates heart and soul passion on the physical plane and beyond... beyond imagination, words and everything that is known.*' Barbara Franken

'*There are many books that discuss one author's road to Enlightenment. But readers want to join the party and experience it for themselves. This book straddles both worlds. While personal, it also expands the topic and makes it interesting, intriguing and achievable.*' Linda A. Lavid, award-winning author.

First published in Great Britain in 2015 by Barbara Franken

© 2015 Barbara Franken

Paperback Edition
ISBN 978-84-606-8793-1
FIRST PAPERBACK EDITION

9 1 2 8 7 3 6 4 5 0

Also available as an eBook
ISBN 978-84-606-7967-7
A CIP Catalogue record of this book is available from the British Library

Published by Barbara Franken
Printed in England by The Lightning Source Group

Your Magnificent Self…

A Journey to Freedom

by

Barbara Franken

2015

Welcome

Welcome to this tranquil and loving space I have created within this book… Your Magnificent Self… A Journey to Freedom that I dedicate to you… the one whose heart feels the gentle stir from within and resonates with my journey… inspiring you to explore, discover and realise your own truth, to enable you to live your grandest dream here on Earth.

Please be aware… your mind will probably not understand much of my journey, but don't worry, be happy and allow your heart to open and resonate with the energy that goes beyond all that is known.

I grew up feeling different and wanting an answer to my deep and burning question… *Who AM I?* I knew there was something more to life than my five senses, a 9 to 5 job and marrying the boy down the road. At the first opportunity I followed my inner passion to explore the truth and left my birth country to begin a journey of discovery.

My book is a unique and magical journey discovering the truth of *Who I AM… Love… and Freedom.* Along my journey I meet nine Elemental Beings, all aspects of myself that help *get me out of my mind* and into my heart and change my life forever. IAM reminded of my core truths that allow me to go beyond my limited Human identity and reality, into a timeless and loving space of *All That Is.*

In this loving space I receive gifts of Love, Passion, Joy, Wisdom and Creativity from all my Selves and become aware of the presence of my Divine self… who waits patiently for my Human self to Awaken and be aware of the Integration and Enlightenment that is naturally unfolding within and allows me to choose to be *free.*

IAM Barbara Franken… Divine Human Master Creator
Inspiring New Energy Consciousness

Contents

Barbara… The End is a New Beginning

"The End is…
Always an opportunity to choose and
experience something new for Self."

Gentle refreshing waves lap over my feet as I enjoy walking along the ocean shore, my feet caress the fine white sparkling sand as they gently sink into the Earth. I smell the fresh seaweed lying on the sand that has naturally drifted ashore, waiting for me to pick it up and lay in my basket. I look out into the transparent and turquoise ocean and see the rich and colourful coral reefs in the depths below, the fish swimming in and out of their home and playground and the dolphins taking their morning swim in the shallow waters.

The ocean is pure and clear, heavy with its natural salt, refreshing and cleansing everything that comes into contact with it. The sun has just risen; the rays gently warm my body and a circle of fluffy white clouds slowly dissolve into a bright blue sky above me, the early rain having fed the luscious nature. I hear the delightful melody of the birds, animals and sea creatures chanting a welcome to this new day as I take my early morning walk and collect my daily treat of fresh seaweed.

IAM on my way back home, which lies not far from the ocean shore, a natural stone cottage in a small village that is scattered amongst the majestic rocks and mountains, tall ancient palm trees, colourful long grasses and large vibrant flowers. My colourful silk dress and long copper hair blow gently in the breeze, shimmering and reflecting the light. I feel the sun warm on my soft olive skin. I feel grand and magnificent, a jubilant joy oozing from me as IAM conscious of being in this moment and this wonderful bright and happy Environment. I breathe a relaxed and contented breath and am thankful for the gentle integration that has occurred within my crystalline DivineHuman self.

IAM eighty years old and remember being around the age of fifty-five when my aging process stood still and my skin began to take on a new elasticity that allow only my laughter lines to appear when I smile and laugh. I feel as youthful as a teenager and my old limited and controlled way of thinking has gently faded away.

The life I have created for myself, here on this wonderful New Earth, allows me to experience many amazing sensations and potential that far reaches anything I could ever have imagined or begin to express.

It is my family's turn to host and light the morning fire, for all those who want to come together for a morning feast in celebration of the new day. Everyone will bring their favourite food and refreshing drink, natural products from the land and sea to share with each other. My father will be bringing his guitar and play delightful melodies, accompanied by my mother and sister's angelic voices. Others will join in, singing songs of heartfelt joy. There will be time this morning to share new potentials, new technologies and new experiences that have been recently discovered and just before our celebration ends, we will spend some *quiet me-time*, consciously breathing together, balancing our Body Consciousness; aligning ourselves with our own consciousness within, the Heavens above, the Earth below and the immediate Environment surrounding us.

How so different life is now. The Earth's Environment sparkles with a pure crystalline light, the reflection of each Divine and Human passion, energies of pure beauty and sensual love that fill each living person and emanate out into the Environment.

One heart at a time, Humankind had awoken to the truth of their own magnificence as they chose to hear their own Divine voice and play out their desire to live and experience a life of freedom, unity and compassion. Each person had recognised their own IAM presence and the wisdom and love they had naturally distilled from their own long Human experience.

Never before had this been done on Earth, we were the new standards of Spirit Incarnate, Embodied and Enlightened, Grand Master Creators of an ever-abundant life. Creating wondrous creations born in freedom, as each person trusted their own Sovereign passion to bring about the most perfect potential and experience desired.

All of us, who knew the truth of our own magnificence and

chose no longer to be held captive in the limited reality of fear and lack, had gradually moved out of the inner cities and into areas of countryside, ocean and lakeshores. To begin a new peaceful life filled with inspiration, imagination and creation. We were still part of the physical Earth and observed the on going conflict, horrific deaths, destruction of the inner cities and the rising fear as religion and politics continued to play out the scenario of *Winner Takes It All*. But simultaneously we were creating and living on a parallel New Earth, a life based on love. We were fulfilling our new role as DivineHumanBeing and experiencing a most magnificent life.

The old foundations and systems of power were gradually collapsing, causing much panic, depression and disease, but consciousness was naturally expanding and allowed many others to see our new way of living and chose to join us. We didn't have to be afraid of the ones who continued to play with the dark and fearful energies, because they couldn't see us, they remained focused on playing in their small world, allowing fear to rule life and conflict and dis-ease to determine their end.

It had been a grand dream we had all held dear for so long and our transformation had happened quite naturally and gracefully, perhaps quite strange to the old Human mind to even think it could be possible. Expanding out of the limited mind and physical reality of time and space, into an ever-expanding reality of no time and infinite space. We created and experienced the unfolding of a New Energy Consciousness, our new home on New Earth, right here on the physical Earth.

When everyone had either finished playing out their Human role and passed over, or chose to join us living in our new expanded Consciousness on New Earth… did the physical Earth and New Earth merge together as One. The pure crystalline structure of the New Earth absorbed the physical Earth and gave birth to a New Crystalline Physical Earth, a multi-physical space of New Energy Consciousness for the DivineHumanBeing and Master Creator to experience expressing and creating their heart and soul's passion.

We are all Sovereign Master Creators who have chosen to allow *All That Is* to serve us in our own way. We are all great leaders who use our unique qualities and joys to create together a Worldwide Co-operation to sustain us all. It is an open and transparent network in which each person shares their own unique creative art form… in business, discovery, innovation, play, education and information worldwide.

Our consciousness attracts the free and abundant energy, which powers our New Earth. We have clean water, clean air, fertile soil, food, drink, clothes and gifts in abundance for everyone to share and enjoy. We are no longer dependent on nature, animals or other people and now enjoy everything. We have no need for money because we each value ourselves and this attracts whatever we want to come into our life.

We don't need relationships, but some of us choose to have them, in particular to enjoy the sweet surrender and ultimate sensual and physical lovemaking. We connect with new souls that want to come in and experience the sensual and free life on New Earth, agreeing to bring them in through the natural human conception of love and the birth process and nurture them for a short while before they feel ready to live independently and fulfil their own role as Master Creator. We are all vibrant, healthy and well and choose when we have experienced enough and are ready to leave the Earth to go on our next adventure.

We no longer need to think or believe; instead we are aligned with our innate knowingness and our distilled human wisdom (from our vulnerabilities, feelings, passions, hopes and dreams, the suffering, injustice, naivety, innocence, fragility, grace and compassion) that guides us on our journey through life in each moment. We each choose where to live, in our own self-sustained home and go about our daily life as we feel fit in each moment. We communicate from the heart and honour and respect all. We are each fully responsible for our words, actions and life situations and our Body Consciousness (the integration of our crystallised Divine light body and mind, our Human physical body and mind and our aspects) is self sustained.

We are grateful for all our Human life experiences and now enjoy experiencing our own Creative Mastery and Enlightenment. We allow our creations to expand and express themself in total freedom… in this way we ensure that our Environment continues to reflect back to us the truth of our freedom, abundance and magnificence.

I have returned home and taken the fresh seaweed to the buffet table that is nicely filling up with mouth-watering foods. We don't need to eat for our physical nourishment anymore, the conscious breath is enough to nourish and sustain our crystalline light body and mind, but we do enjoy consciously tasting small amounts of quality foods and drinks. I welcomed all my friends and family who were arriving to share precious and sacred time and enjoyed a wonderful morning celebration together, singing, talking, consciously breathing, eating and drinking, giving thanks… to the existence of Self… to the new day… to the fire of creation… and to our family and friendships.

We shared the left over food and drink to take back home, stacked the chairs back against a low wall behind the buffet table and we all began to go our separate ways back home or out to work or play. The fire was smouldering low; I walked across and lifted some sand with my bare feet to dampen the flames. My parents who were now in their early hundred's came to kiss me farewell before making their own way home, a short walk away. My sister, husband and children came to embrace my family before leaving and continuing their day.

The day was once again mine to enjoy. Tom was heading off to town to gather with some new students who wanted to bring their new discovery into the open market place. Our children and grand children were leaving for a local exploration, looking for new colours and textures to make new paints for their Creative Art Business. I wandered across the lawn and into our home. I was working on a new project, helping my quantum physic friends implement the *free energy* generators that would connect all our technology in each home and work space. Documents and drawings covered my creative table that stood in the middle of my workspace; a tranquil room situated at the far end of our cottage.

Like the rest of our home, I had designed my workspace and sanctuary to be simple, relaxing and spacious. My favourite paintings hung on the walls, serene figurines stood in the corners and my creative cupboard full of collected treasures, stood tall and proud on the back wall behind a most comfortable sofa where I would spend my time relaxing and daydreaming. It had taken me two years to coordinate the designing, building and decorating of our home. It was a delightful natural stone cottage with grand arched open doors and windows with sills full of giant trailing red roses. From the outside the cottage looked quite small, but inside it was truly grand. The entrance hall was showered with my colourful SoulArt paintings and beautiful figurines. Three beautiful archways led to two master bedrooms with large en-suites and walk-in wardrobes and a large open living space divided up into three distinct areas.

Sunlight flooded the spacious area and beautiful golden voile curtains gently swayed at the sides of the open windows. On the right was our kitchen, simple, natural and modern with plenty of cupboard space and all the latest gadgets to make cooking easy and fun. In the corner was a small pantry where we kept all the fresh foods cool and dry. Cooking was one of my creative passions, creating the aromas and different tastes for myself and family and friends to enjoy.

The kitchen led into an open dining space where a long wooden table and six comfy chairs stood in front of a large glass dresser displaying our crystal and china ware. Two pedestals, adorned with beautiful arrays of flowers stood on the left hand side, separating the sitting room that occupied the other side of the room. In the centre of the sitting room was an open fireplace with comfortable, soft sofas and small coffee tables encircling it at different angles.

At one end of the room was our entertainment screen that

connected to live worldwide performances of sport, dance, music and theatre. It was also a direct feed to everyone's information, discoveries and creations that everyone shared. It was only because everything and everyone was now open, transparent and truthful about themself that this interconnection was possible. Everyone's choice as to what they wanted to share or be kept private was honoured at all times. At the other end of the room the wall was full of our family photographs, a display of our favourite books and on the floor was a colourful treasure chest, full of toys and games to play with the children. Another beautiful archway on the back wall led out to a bathroom and two tranquil workspaces.

Where IAM now, tidying up my project table before relaxing on my sofa with the book I published many moons ago. A true and unique story discovering Love and Freedom for myself. I recall my magical experience perceiving nine Elemental Beings, aspects and potentials of myself, coming back, one by one to join and guide me gracefully through the natural awakening and integration of my Human and Divine selves. They helped me feel and experience the potential and love I truly AM… in the physical reality and beyond… preparing me to experience my Enlightenment as an Embodied DivineHuman Being.

It was with much gratitude to everyone who had inspired me, that I wanted to share my extra-ordinary and magnificent life experience with others, to inspire them to choose freedom for themself and experience who they truly are.

What a magnificent and abundant life the writing and publishing of my book continued to attract. Not only did my book become one of the best 'Self-Realisation and Awareness' books of 2015, but for many years it inspired people to open their heart, integrate with their Divine Self and expand into the timeless freedom, experiencing their own Magnificent Master Creator self.

Magdalena… Loving Self First

"Loving Self First is…
To focus and connect with the LOVE IAM, to be self
full and be able to feel safe, cherished,
clear and balanced."

My awakening journey began at the age of eighteen when I made the bold move to leave my family home in England and travel overseas. I eventually settled in Holland where I began to focus, explore and discover myself and my life in great depth and detail. It was not until my husband Tom and I moved to a peaceful and tranquil part of Southern Spain, that I truly began to relax and open fully to the natural world, the present moment and my core truths. These truths were made clear to me in the form of nine Elemental Beings that I began to perceive and receive messages from. They were all aspects of me, separated during many lifetimes on Earth… but now I had chosen to bring all parts of myself back together as One Body Consciousness.

During one of my quiet me-times I invited all my aspects to come back and join me in this now physical reality. I didn't have to wait long before I perceived my first Elemental Being and the beginning of seven magical and intense years began.

Our home and garden in Spain is a most tranquil and magical place I have ever known, it is situated within a cluster of colourful and elegant homes, scattered in a mountainous valley of citrus fruit trees not far from the Mediterranean sea. For most of the year we live outside, lazing under the blue skies that stretch above us giving the sun ample opportunity to shine its light and warmth. There is nothing but a silent hum of nature in the air and as I relax in the shade on my sunbed or go about my creative pursuits under the gazebo, I listen to the birds and bees sing sweetly as they go about their day and the palm trees and flowers gently rustle in the breeze that seem to encourage the flowers to open up and emanate a wonderful fragrance.

I see Dragonflies, butterflies and fairies too; flying around the tall green plants, my crystal garden, colourful flowers, zigzagging over the pool water and diving in now and again for a mouthful of cool water fulfilling their natural earthly tasks. The light of the sun bounces off the pool leaving sparkling crystal lights dancing on the water, inviting me in for a cool swim and share the joy of the natural world.

I find it all delightful, listening to nature's song in between the serene silence, my own conscious breath, the notes of a bird's song, the fluttering of insects and the wind blowing its breeze. It brings me to a deep and serene place within the core of life itself, into a pool of nothingness. It is in this space that I begin to feel a loving presence stir deep within me, expanding throughout my entire body and outside of myself. It is as if someone is hugging me from the inside, all my cells are vibrating in a gentle and colourful delight. I feel a deep and warm knowing of being cherished and safe and can imagine someone gently whispering loving words into which I surrender to.

I ask myself what this loving feeling is and understand that it is my true Divine and timeless self naturally unfolding and integrating with my Human self. I imagine a beautiful guardian angel, Magdalena sitting beside me, rocking me back and forth. She has come to share her loving wisdom with me. Magdalena explains that she is the part of me that radiates pure love throughout my being and beyond, a timeless consciousness of light that emanates my true sovereignty and magnificence from within. IAM an amazing beauty that could feel safe knowing that no one, Human, Spirit or Alien would ever waste their time intruding or playing games with such a loving and beautiful presence.

She tells me that love is where I have come from, what IAM and where IAM going. I emerged from a pure source of love that is inseparable from my physical Human body and mind. It is now time to be aware and allow my Divine self to fully integrate with my Human self, to allow the release of my ancestral biology and past lifetimes of pain and suffering and allow myself to experience the passion and love of my Divine essence and the sensual joy and wisdom from my Humanness.

Magdalena would accompany me everywhere I went for many

years to come, even flying under the airplane when I travelled across the seas. She would expand her wings, stretching out both sides to eternity to help make me feel safe. When she wanted to share her teachings of love, I would feel a shudder of excited passion flow through my body and hear her urgent voice, reminding me to breathe consciously. She taught me how important it was to question myself, and my life and be clear about what I wanted, what I desired to experience and have in my life. She encouraged me to open myself up to *All That IAM*, to pursuit my creativity and listen for the discrete but all knowing answers from within and without.

I practice regularly the conscious breath, connect with my Divine essence and IAM presence and feel into the pool of pure love and passion that I truly AM. I allow myself to expand into *All of myself*, going beyond my personality, fears and insecurities and feel the grace of who I truly AM at my core.

Magdalena told me that the pure loving essence of my Divine self expands throughout my whole being and out into the world and is what attracts my heart and soul's passion and desire into my physical reality. But, until IAM more aware of the *energy dynamics* and allow myself to embrace and release all my past wounds and fears that have become very much part of my mind and personality, it is my Human thoughts and emotions that attract life to me and keep me in the game.

She told me how important it is to feel into the Environment, people, and situations I find myself in. I could expand my Body Consciousness (*All of myself...* Body, Mind and Spirit) out into a space, imagining I have antenna that can feel around me and pick up signals as to whether or not something resonates with me. In this way I can allow the love and joy I feel to guide me on my journey.

Magdalena instilled within me the wisdom of how important it is for me to love myself first and foremost. Something society has not encouraged anyone to do, in fact has taught that it is selfish and wrong to put our Self before others. As a society we have learnt how to make others feel happy and secure, but this only left us yearning for love within ourselves… and our search to find someone else to love us and make us feel complete began. It was time to change this old teaching and she asked me to look at what I thought it meant to *truly love* and apply it to myself.

I came up with the following points that are important to me…

- *To be compassionate with myself, by simply being present, loving, accepting and embracing everything about myself without judgment, pity or trying to fix myself.*
- *To give myself quiet me-time's in which to relax and reflect on my self and my life.*
- *To see the perfection in all my weakness and all my strength.*
- *To be my own best friend.*
- *To eat according to my body's desire, to dress uniquely and grand, to be present with my head held high and my magnificent smile of joy.*
- *To be actively creative, have fun, play and explore.*
- *To allow myself to express how I truly feel in each moment.*
- *To allow myself to be happy, healthy, wealthy and vibrant.*
- *To be around people I admire and enjoy being with.*

Only when I can allow myself to be all of these things, completely loving and owning *All of myself*, is it possible to be ready to choose to live a life of love, joy and grace and experience the delight of Embodied Enlightenment.

True Love is… to be there for myself… always… no exception.

Human experience is a great playground for everyone to learn how to care and nurture Self… to pay attention, to be aware, to honour, to respect, to be unique, to find our own space and find out what we like and don't like. We all have so much potential and opportunity within Self to lead us to our freedom… and live our life as we desire.

I find that caring, liking and loving *All of myself* is quite a new concept, but gradually, with practice it is becoming quite natural to put myself first. I have begun to enjoy going outside on my own to sit quietly or dance under the sun and the moon where I feel as if IAM discovering a new friend. I connect to nature's rhythm and embrace *All of myself...* and IAM finding my own unique beat. I feel it is truly a most wonderful time, discovering new depths of feelings, compassion and being present in the world around me. It gives me a cherished, loving and secure feeling within me, which seems to radiate out into the world and makes it possible for me to care for others in a truly compassionate way.

During the latter part of the year being so close with Magdalena, I perceived her breasts growing bigger and before I knew it she had given birth to Cordelia. She had fulfilled her teaching role with me and now it was time for her to nurture her own daughter and bring her through infancy and childhood. The time seemed to fly by so very quickly, they both came by to check on me now and again and I was always amazed how quickly Cordelia was growing up.

With my new found love and compassion for myself I often wandered out into the open countryside where I lived, admiring the barren land that seemed long forgotten; except for nature's wild flowers and a multitude of rocks that covered the desert ground. I sensed the energy around me, from the earth and heaven, vibrating high with much love and joy.

Early one morning, when I was dowsing the land just outside my home for vital energy centres, I perceived the presence of a very long legged gentle being, striding up and down the land in big soft paces. He seemed to be very busy with what ever he was doing, but simultaneously I perceived him walking close beside me, explaining to me the importance of the land; of the vital energy centres and ley lines that connected everything together, allowing energy or information to flow and nourish the land.

Jeremy… Loving and Nurturing the Environment

**"Loving and Nurturing the Environment is…
To be responsible for caring and loving
Self because IAM the Environment."**

During one of my early Intuitive Painting workshops at my home, I clearly asked myself at the beginning of an opening inner journey, what my new long legged friend looked like and what he wanted to be called. So it came as no surprise when I intuitively painted Jeremy… a very tall long legged man with long blond hair around his head and face and immaculately dressed in grand and colourful sovereign clothes.

Similar to my relationship with Magdalena, Jeremy allowed me to perceive him so that I could open up to the wisdom with regards to nurturing our Environment and Mother Earth. He walked by my side, inspiring me as I worked the community barren land with my friends on Mazarron Country Club, transforming it into beautiful gardens. Jeremy instilled in me a love for nurturing the Environment and everything that was part of it… the soil, rocks, plants, trees, animals and people.

During my outings; exploring different regions of Spain, he suggested that I gather different types of rocks and bring them back home to decorate the gardens. After a few years, I noticed that some of the rocks were changing appearance and I became curious as to what was happening to them as well as to why Jeremy continuously walked up and down the land as he did.

He explained to me that the land contains an enormous amount of salts and minerals that create a pure and clear crystalline structure in which to absorb the raw powerful and creative energy that flows vertically down from the heavens, through the mountain peaks and into the vortexes; circular points on the Earth surface, where they meet the raw energies of the Earth that flow upward. The coming together of the Heavenly and Earthly energies is a great love affair… transforming the raw energies into life force energy that flow horizontally through the ley lines and nurture the whole landscape.

Not only where I lived, but all over the world, in our pursuit to be rich and powerful, Humankind had stripped the Earth of her natural resources. Blocking her nurturing process by flattening her natural mountain peaks to build our homes, chopping down her rain forests to make our comforts, blocking the natural flow of her rivers to gain land, stealing her oils and jewels for profit and polluting her skies in our travels.

Mother Earth is a living and breathing organism that needs to be nurtured and protected from our Human greed, ignorance and poor planning. Jeremy had begun to help the Earth quicken her pace of nurturing the landscape on the Country Club. Each of his footprints consciously vibrating love deep down inside the Earth's core, carrying a message of unconditional love and a promise to help her at this most critical time.

The Earth eagerly responded to this by opening up her vital energy centres and mountain peaks and the *reunion* of the powerful raw energies allowed the nurturing of the landscape to vibrate... like never before.

Slowly and quite naturally, as Humankind becomes more and more aware of their connection to *all*, the Earth and all her life form opens up and takes on a new higher vibration, a crystalline vibration of pure and clear love. Everyone can choose to feel into this transformation, simply by allowing their consciousness to expand beyond their known physical reality and become aware of an unknown multi-sensual reality that exists simultaneously in the present moment.

Eventually the unknown permeates into the known physical world and this is the change I have noticed happening to the rocks as they transform into their crystalline Self.

I wanted others to see and understand this magnificent happening and began collecting the beautiful crystalline rocks from around our gardens and made a grand piece of Earth SoulArt, a crystal mandala that outlined one of the larger vortexes that I had earlier dowsed with my sacred friends.

Jeremy reminded me that our Human body and mind is not excluded from this natural transformation that is taking place on Earth. Through our conscious breath we are receiving the intense light energy from our solar system and beyond and the loving Earth energy from deep within the Earth that saturates our atoms and cells causing them to take on a new higher crystalline vibration.

The Human physical body and mind is taking a natural quantum leap into its own Divinity. The pure and clear crystalline light of Divine love and intelligence itself is absorbing the physical body and mind and integrating into One Body Consciousness.

This natural transformation process causes the physical body and mind to re-structure and re-balance. Old ways and patterns to be rewired and re-written and hidden dark aspects of Self, shaken lose. It makes people feel raw, chaotic and unbalanced at times, especially if they remain unaware of what is happening and don't realise that this is all part of a natural cycle of change. Many people become unwell and enter the depths of depression.

If a person is lucky, the illness takes them into a void, a wonderful opportunity for some quiet me-time, to connect to a part of them self that is pure love and a knowing that everything is OK. With the conscious breath they can expand within themself, feel into their own true nature and be aware of who they truly are.

Jeremy suggested that I read a book by Bruce Lipton: The Biology of Belief. I read it all one evening into the small hours, as I couldn't put it down; my heart exploding with so many ah ha moments that I literally felt my consciousness expand out into the universe.

As a Cellular Biologist, Bruce discovered in his cell research that we are designed by nature to fit into our Environment, but when we change the Environment too much, we lose our natural balance and change ourselves. Not for the better, but with disease of the body, mind and spirit.

Bruce asks us to imagine our body as a television. (A television that broadcast's a station from somewhere outside us via an aerial). Each person, being unique has their own identity and owns unique antennae (receptors). They are found on the outer membrane of each cell and download a unique and complementary signal from our immediate Environment or from our perception of the Environment and broadcast this through our body and behave accordingly. Bruce went on to explain that even when our body is no longer alive, we continue to broadcast ourselves, as we hear from patients with transplanted organs.

So what exactly did this mean? I exist in accordance with my Environment. My identity is outside of my body, in the Environment. Am I the Environment? Oh my goodness… was science taking a quantum leap confirming what the old Enlightened Masters had always said and what my inner voice had always known?'

The Environment is *All That Is*… so therefore IAM the Environment. IAM Spirit in material form. I adapt to the Environment, respond to life by using my antennae and adjust my biology accordingly. This meant that IAM no victim nor powerless, but indeed all-powerful, I change my genetic pattern as I experience, respond and change in life.

Jeremy reminds me how important it is to take quiet me-time, which enables me to connect with the quietness, both within myself, and my Environment. IAM a good student and connect daily with the natural world.

- *I listen to the hum of the earth and connect with Mother Earth and feel her vibration.*
- *I caress her as I take each conscious step, sending my love down to her core.*
- *I open myself up to the natural song and dance of the Earth and the Heavens that IAM part of too.*
- *I allow everything to be, not labelling a tree a tree or a rock a rock, but just allow everything to be as it is.*
- *I open myself to receive the unconditional love from the Earth and the Heavens, allowing nature to calm and inspire me.*
- *I observe nature's natural cycles and allow myself to be a part of her rhythm.*

Jeremy brought my attention to Fractal Geometry and Fibonacci and the Golden Ratio that shows the structural unity and harmony of our natural world. Patterns, no matter their micro or macro size, are all similar when we look deeper into life and find the core symmetry. One of the most basic constants in the universe is the golden ratio or phi .6180 that grows in perfect proportion. The increase in the size of the joints of our fingers and toes towards our palm and foot and the similarities of the branches of our trees, leafs, rivers and human capillaries, DNA and organs in our body. Each pattern of nature shows its interconnectedness with *all* and its infinity representing infinite wholeness and the truth of *All That Is.*

I spend many hours researching and pondering the patterns of nature and how this connected with my life and the natural awakening and shift of consciousness that is taking place on Earth at this time. What I find inspires me to create, together with my sacred friends… Anna-Marie, Gill, Julia, Mary and Wendy… Project Magnificent Consciousness. A visualisation of our feelings and how we feel we can create a world of Love, Peace and Community. (Our artwork and write up is displayed on the following pages).

We exhibit our Art Project in a local school, restaurant and town hall that inspires others, especially children at school to talk about their dreams and passions and create their own colourful artwork. I visualise this contagiously spreading around the whole world.

Jeremy remains very loyal to me, walking by my side, even joining Magdalena and myself on our trips across the seas. He instills within me the deep connection that IAM everything, which always brings me much peace and understanding.

At a certain point Cordelia turns twenty-one, she is a very beautiful young angel and appears to me when IAM feeling sad, doubtful or caught up in life's drama. She comes to remind me that it isn't necessary to play the Human games anymore and feel this way. Instead I can trust myself completely and know everything is OK. I can relax and observe the games we all play and accept them as the experience they are and part of a much bigger picture.

Sensing the Natural Order
Cycles & Beauty of Mother Earth

In this first section of our Art Project we imagine Humankind awakening to sense...

- *The beauty and sacredness of the natural world*
- *The natural order and perfection of all life*
- *The positive and negative that make up the whole of life*
- *The natural cycles of birth and death*
- *The underlying Energy that is the foundation of all life*
- *The interconnection, interdependence & uniqueness within the oneness*
- *The unique and magnificent part Humankind plays in life*

Individual Awakening
of Who We Truly Are

In this second section of our Art Project we imagine a world where each individual…

- *Knows that everything begins and ends with themself*
- *Makes peace with all parts of themself*
- *Loves themself completely and unconditionally*
- *Dares to live their grandest dream*
- *Is the change they want to see in the world*
- *Becomes one with their Divine essence*
- *Realises freedom and embraces all of life*

We are Creators of our Reality, Creating our Hearts Desire… Living in Cooperation, Peace, Joy & Harmony with **ALL**

In this third section of our Art Project we imagine a world full of DivineHumanBeings who…

- *Know of their true Magnificence and Sovereign IAM Self*
- *Live a sensual life of ease and grace*
- *Live with clarity and knowingness*
- *Are free to express and create their heart and soul's desire*
- *Honour the reverence of all life*
- *Live in harmonious cooperation with others*
- *Allow a new crystalline physical body and mind to be birthed… here on Earth*

Cordelia... Trusting Self Completely

**"Trusting Self is...
To feel and know that everything
is OK and live my life... my way."**

Now and again I find myself caught up in the drama and trauma of life and the game of energy feeding that unfortunately, has become the normal practice for most people within family and friendships at home and at work. We play the different roles of victim, aggressor and rescuer… stealing each other's energy… gaining and losing power. It makes us feel important, right and just by making another feel useless, wrong and not good enough.

My generation has been brought up to care about what people think of us, how we fit into society and how to behave in the world. We should be nice and polite, not hurt anyone and follow the rules. No wonder I have always needed other people's approval, recognition and attention. Like so many, I had not been taught that I have a mind of my own, IAM a unique individual, important and of value, have feelings and desires of my own. IAM quite able to give myself love and attention, be responsible for everything in my life and stand out and express… Hello… here IAM.

I was about thirty-five before I realised that I didn't have to fight or cry for attention or have the need to be recognised by others. Thankfully, through my own life experiences I have gradually become aware that I can recognise my own uniqueness, value and importance, take my stand and express myself as I wish in each moment.

When I feel sad, doubtful or occasionally in the depths of self-pity, Cordelia comes to comfort me and lovingly reminds me that love is what IAM made of, that IAM whole, unique, innocent and extremely important. She told me to read the story of Joan of Arc… instilling in me that it is my time now. IAM a powerful force too and there is nothing that can ever hurt or deter me. I don't have to give in to indoctrination, bullying, fear and control from anything outside myself.

She told me about the new times that are upon us now and

how I can choose to trust myself, not in a forceful way but by simply choosing to observe myself in life. Choosing how I want my life to be... unlimited, free and flexible, releasing all control, living out of my mind, with an open heart and innate intelligence. Choosing to be magnificent, grand, to have a healthy body, abundant riches and passionate. Choosing to go beyond my programmed and limited mind, body and physical reality and expand into *All That Is*.

IAM courageous and embrace *All of myself* even the broken, hurt and dark fearful parts of me. Yes, through the conscious breath I can bring all the parts of myself, that I have hidden or thrown away, back home and allow them to move through my physical body and express themself before their ultimate release and transformation into new potential.

I know it is in my best interest for me to leave the old world of energy feeding, duality and conflict behind me. Cordelia told me it is a question of trusting myself, knowing that I will be OK and able to move on to experience being truly safe and alive in my own right.

- *To trust my mind to know all my answers to my questions.*
- *To trust my body to balance, rebuild and rejuvenate itself.*
- *To trust my spirit essence, my Divine self to guide me on my journey of adventure and exploration beyond everything known.*

I observe my actions in relationship to others and become more aware that trusting myself is to stay true to myself and not compromise my values and truth. I observe how I feel and understand what is right and good for me in each moment and chose it for myself. I feel into the energies when in company, trusting if I feel comfortable or uncomfortable with people. I discern what energy is mine and what is not, choosing to release everything that isn't mine or no longer serves me and claim ownership for what is mine. I trust that all energy I release, either returns to its original owner or is transmuted into a pure and neutral energy, filled with potential for me to use at my discretion.

One significant observation I make is the way I judge myself and others so critically. I hear quite clearly my ego voice say... 'This doesn't look quite right'... 'This isn't good'... 'This needs to be changed'... 'Everyone's going to notice'... 'I don't want to look like this'... 'What are others going to think'... and on and on the voice goes. Even when IAM out relaxing or eating my meal in public, I will people watch and my ego voice appears and scrutinizes critically... 'Don't they know how to dress properly'? 'Their hair looks funny'... 'Fancy coming out like that'... 'They can't walk in those shoes'.

'Oh my goodness... AM I always behaving like this?' IAM still participating in the Human game of this is good and this is bad, with my ego talk going on in the background as if it is normal. But I know it is never too late and as I slowly become more aware of my words and actions, I naturally change my behaviour. It is just a matter of trusting the process... trusting myself to accept my own appearance and accept the choice others make on their own journey. If I don't like something about myself, or an experience, IAM clear about what I desire and change it if I can or wait in acceptance for the physical time-gap to catch up with my intention... and in the meantime I become one with my personal dislike and embrace the experience without separation.

My mind continues to seduce me back into the game, sometimes it wins but sometimes I choose to accept myself as IAM.

I recognise my consciousness as the observer of my Human behaviour. My compassionate Divine presence being aware of my Human mind and ego identity that is trying to take possession of me. My ego identity has certainly lived up to her character name... Ms Miserable, dwelling on negative and fearful past experience and projecting them into my future. At times her constant chattering makes it hard for me to focus or experience anything new or positive but practicing my deep conscious breath brings quietness into the equation and I experience longer pauses of silence.

In the silence I can hear the compassionate voice of Ms Amazing, my Divine self, who loves and trusts herself no matter what. She knows the past is only an experience; energy mostly projected onto me by others and is no longer relevant.

Cordelia told me that it is easy to allow my emotional and physical pains to call the shots and bring me into a downward spiral of unease and self-pity, allowing Ms Miserable to possess my body, mind and spirit. But it isn't necessary, instead I can become one with *what is*, accept and surrender my fight; at the same time, I can be clear of what I want to experience and trust that Ms Amazing will bring it into my life at the most appropriate time.

Trust, changes the energy dynamics and allows me to be aware of the expanding space of Ms Amazing and be able to smile... Just because the sun shines... Just because the rain pours... Just because I can see... hear... taste... feel... smell... Just because I can get up in the morning... Just because I can choose... and suddenly it happens... I begin to notice my emotional and physical pain disappearing into the background and the love of Ms Amazing brightening all of my days.

I remember Adamus in one of the Crimson Circle monthly Shouds explaining that the mind wants nothing more than to go beyond and integrate with its Divine knowingness. In the meantime I just have to accept and embrace my ego voice and eventually it will become quiet, expand and become one with my Body Consciousness.

To help me come to a better understanding of the darker aspects of myself, Cordelia helped me remember the truths about the hurts and wounds of Humankind...

All parents, teachers and friends have strong and weak points that children take on as their own and allow them self to feel hurt... until they recognise that this is not who they are and release the energy back to its original state.

People intentionally hurt each other because they feel trapped in life and lash out at others. This action leaves great feelings of remorse, and as each person is their own judge and jury condemn themself to dark quarters... *'IAM unworthy'*... *'IAM a bad person'*... *'I can't control my anger'*... until we recognise that this is only part of the whole story and only an experience to help us understand our responsibility in creating circumstances and taking consequences in life.

Cordelia encourages me to embrace all my *unhappy* aspects of unworthiness, feeling bad and angry and allow them to become part of me, releasing them from their eternal torment. She went on to explain that for a long time Humans had felt a woundedness and disconnection around mothers. No matter what happened in my past, my mother, like all mothers, had done her very best and I could respect and honour her for her deeds towards me because within each deed she had left an element of love that I could own and nurture for myself.

Once I recognise this seed of love, deeply hidden within all action and non-action in my relationships, I can understand that each experience is essentially about loving, whether difficult or easy, it is an experience for me to discover love for myself. I can then become the experience, own it, mould it and nurture it for myself. This new awareness of love dissolves and releases all my past wounds and I wouldn't have to ask myself *'How can I love myself more'*... *'Why don't I love myself'*... or *'What do I need to love myself'* because I would know that the seed of love is within me, waiting patiently for me to nurture it.

Expanding into my own LOVE
With a nice deep breath... I allow the seed of love to expand within and without me and resonate with the energy of Mother Earth... allowing her love, abundance and the present moment to flow through my whole being... I feel at peace and know that everything is perfectly well as it always is.

It is time for me to feel into *All That Is*, the place where I come from and where IAM now and always will be. Cordelia encourages me to continue my quiet me-times where I can practice my conscious breath and connect to my deep commitment to know my Divine essence. To expand beyond *All That I Know* and trust myself (even if my mind doesn't make sense of it) to let go of everything that no longer serves me and be free to be myself.

An Expanded Journey into All That Is

Relaxing and breathing consciously with my eyes closed... feeling out into all the cosmos and within myself... feeling the infinite depth and interconnected web of energy that All life is... It is a space where my Divine essence lives in complete wholeness, beyond my physical senses and All that is known and limited...

Taking some deep conscious breaths I allow myself to expand out of my awareness of my physical self and into an unknown space... only feeling and breathing... allowing myself to experience everything and nothing... whatever there is to experience or not experience... as there is no right way to experience because everything is unique... just breathing and feeling... allowing my mind to come in and out with its chatter... until it becomes still...

I visualise my Divine essence as light dancing joyfully in and out of two realities (the known and the unknown)... flowing in harmonious waves... in and out... and then they touch... my Divine light touches my physical self... I feel an energy of love flow through my body... and the two come together in a joyous embrace... energies so pure becoming one within All That Is... only feeling and breathing... experiencing it all... experiencing the beginning of a most magnificent love affair with myself...

Jake… Understanding, Accepting and Integrating

"Integrating is…
Understanding and accepting All of Self and All of life
and allowing everything IAM to come back and be
One Body Consciousness."

The more I love, trust and allow myself to be free from all my yesterdays and past lives, the more free I feel to open up and expand into a new understanding and acceptance of *All of myself* and *All of life*. Ah ha moments continue to bubble up from deep within me, new insights expand my consciousness and deepen the connection I have to *All That Is*.

It is during one of my expanded journeys, expanding beyond the physical realm into *All That Is*, that Jake an original wild squirrel with magnificent wings appears by my side and introduces himself. He has come to accompany me on new journeys into different realms and dimensions and expand my consciousness further into the unknown. Jake is here to help me bring all parts and aspects of myself back home, where everything belongs and will make me whole and balanced.

Our first journey together is back through time to visit all my past history, not to dig up forgotten times, but to release all the experiences and potentials that I haven't yet chosen to experience. I take a conscious walk with Jake into the hallway of my past, my history and all my yesterdays; walking past many doors that hold my unexpressed potential. Potential of love and light, as all the dark and fearful potentials have long since transmuted back into a neutral state. As I walk past each door I choose for it to open, which releases all my potential; all the roles never played out, decisions never made and directions never taken and I invite the potential that is now free, to come back into the now moment for me to use.

Jake explains that we are now living in a New Energy Consciousness, a time where we can easily allow everything to come back to ourselves and be One Body Consciousness. A time to discover we are so much more than we could ever imagine. A time to discover that everything is right here in the now moment and it is no longer necessary to go outside of our self for anything.

Visiting my past made me realise my history is nothing but potential, IAM not only my history, but also so much more. Each lifetime I gave myself a wonderful gift, to choose out of so much potential how I wanted to express myself. Destiny seems to be something we have created to help us understand and play out experiences in the physical reality, but actually destiny doesn't exist, only the choices each of us make. I realise in that moment...

IAM every potential... IAM every expression... IAM plentiful.... IAM multiple... IAM everything... and Life is a field of Potential for me to choose and create my heart and soul's desire.

On my next journey with Jake, I expand into the depths within *All my bodies...* physical, mental, emotional and spiritual; to begin restoration work on my whole communication system that had broken down after many life times of neglect. I expand my awareness and travel into elaborate but simple networks of magnetics, electrics, energy movement, physics and pulses. I become aware of what needs to be done and after our initial inspection I leave Jake to complete the project.

It takes me well over a year to feel clearer in mind, more creative in nature and more confident in my authority. IAM Captain of my own ship, able to choose in each moment which course to sail. My communication network has been restored and *All my bodies* have come together and aligned as One Body Consciousness. I know my Body Consciousness will keep everything in balance from now on and will allow appropriate new potential to come in and attract corresponding energies to rejuvenate my being and allow me the abundance of health, wealth, passion, joy and creativity.

Another journey I take with Jake is into my future. We return to the hallway of my past, but this time I allow the hallway to dissolve, making it possible to walk into myself, to walk into all the potential that I have released from my past. They are all here, but I feel I can go further. I dissolve my walking and allow myself to go past all the facts, beliefs, destiny, past everything known and go into a field beyond everything imaginable. I surround myself with pure and loving potential... the IAM that IAM.

I allow myself to feel into this new field of awareness, expanding my consciousness; allowing myself just to be. I know that this will unlock, activate and open pure new potential in a most magnificent and flowing way into my life. Potential that will fulfil my grandest dream, the dream of my Human self, Creative mind and Divine self, living as One Body Consciousness here in the physical reality.

My expansive journeys with Jake have allowed me to feel glimpses of freedom, to go beyond everything known, beyond the limits of my physical reality, beyond the mind and imagination, beyond the five senses and there is no going back now. I have welcomed home and integrated forgotten parts of myself. IAM the IAM, so much more than I ever thought possible. IAM awakening from what feels like a long deep sleep. I take a deep breath and acknowledge...

I truly AM a self-contained conscious being that uses energy, energy that comes in at the most appropriate time to serve me. I don't need to rely on anything outside of myself; I can love and trust myself completely and create my heart and soul's desire.

Occasionally other people's energy finds its way into my Body Consciousness, triggering Ms Miserable to come out to play with my doubts, anger or irritability. I look at what is happening and embrace my own concerns. I become the doubt, anger or irritability, as I know there is no separation, before the energy releases itself through my conscious breath. I know that if I allow the energy to stay around unacknowledged or resisted, the energy will solidify and cause a blockage in my physical body and eventually cause me physical pain and definitely put a stop to my creative process. An example of how I stopped my creative process happened once on holiday...

I was so happy to arrive on this beautiful island, with its relaxing atmosphere and wonderful food, drink and people. Until the second day when I found the sunbeds on the beach and around the pool in shaded areas were all reserved with pool towels... and unoccupied. People must have come down so early to reserve their place for the day, even when they were not actually using them. The more I thought about it, the more irritated I became and my mood turned sombre. How could so many people behave in such an anti-social and possessive way? What had happened to using the sunbeds only when you needed to?

On the third day all my jolliness had disappeared, I still couldn't find a sunbed in the shade to relax in and by the time evening came, my face and chest was fiery red, not through sunburn but through my irritation. On our way to having our evening cocktails we used an elevator that stopped in-between floors and we were stuck for quite a while. Our evening only seemed to go downhill from there, so we decided it was best to call it a day and retire early. I spent some time reflecting on the last few days and asked myself how I could put an end to this situation and move on. Could I accept that it was normal for people to behave like this?

I took some deep conscious breaths and a question came to mind. 'Where is Ms Amazing who always trusts that energy serves her, no matter what?' Some more conscious breaths and an avalanche of information flowed through me.

I had allowed the inconsiderate action of others to take away my trust and understanding of how life works and this had stopped my creative process. I had allowed their human stride with their own ego... me, me, me... fighting for their rightful place to the detriment of others, to affect me instead of accepting that their action was part of the Human game.

Only when I AM clear about what I desire, no matter the noise that I hear from others around me, can it come into being. If I wanted a sunbed in the shade, I had to allow myself to focus on it and trust that in the most perfect place someone would either just be leaving or there would be an empty space available as I passed by. I felt joy returning to my being and my fiery red body began to calm down. I could now sleep well knowing that everything was OK... tomorrow I would find my perfect shaded space.

Life is about understanding and accepting *All of myself*, and *All of life*. When I look beyond my limited and chaotic mind, it is clear that IAM responsible for all my thoughts and actions that create each experience and situation I find myself in.

Life has its way of reminding me how everything in life works together in harmony. If I don't like a particular experience, I know I have the power to change it. I simply have to be clear and choose again in the moment, this would move the energy and create the potential for something new to come into my life.

Ormus... Energy Dynamics and being the Creator IAM

**"The Grand Creator IAM is...
Being One Body Consciousness, a crystalline
self-contained being, who uses energy to
sustain Self."**

As more and more new information finds its way to me from various sources about New Energy Consciousness the more excited I become and the more information I desire. I feel as if IAM a sponge soaking up information and growing incredibly big... and as if by command Ormus appears into my life during one of my Creative Workshops.

IAM painting intuitively when a blue blob drops off my paintbrush onto the back of a healing card IAM creating and as there are no mistakes whilst painting intuitively; I observe how it gradually transforms into an ancient Elemental animal of great beauty and colour. A few days later when IAM alone, I pick up my healing card and ask him his name and why he is here.

I hear the word OROMUS being whispered in my left ear and that I had best go to my computer and look up the word on the internet. I intuitively know that he has come into my life to help me expand into the knowingness of New Energy Consciousness. IAM familiar with this energy; through my lessons with my extraordinary Dutch teacher Pieter; although we didn't name or label the energy, we only felt into it... and later as a fellow Shambra, affiliated with the Crimson Circle I played with the energy more.

Curiosity takes me to my computer at the first opportunity and I search for the name on the Internet... OROMUS. It is a name given to a group of bugs. *This isn't what IAM looking for'*... and... automatically scrolling down the page, I come across in bold capital letters...

'WHY DON'T YOU LOOK UP THE WORD ORMUS'
How wonderfully spooky this is and with a spring in my fingers I type in the name ORMUS and come across a website www.subtleenergies.com. In awe and eagerness during the next few days, I read through some amazing information that Barry Carter has put together and published about ORMUS research on his website.

ORMUS (or ORMEs... Orbitally Rearranged Monatomic Elements) are natural non-metallic seeds of the metals consisting of one or more atoms in a high spin state giving them unusual properties as superconductivity, superfluidity, supercurrent and magnetic levitation.

ORMUS is the first matter according to ancient alchemists who have referred to them as *noble metals, white powder of god, manna, food of the gods*. They are new forms of matter that have different physical properties than normal elements and can't be detected or explained by conventional chemistry and lab tests. The elements are thought to be as much as 10.000 times more abundant than their corresponding metallic counterparts: Cobalt, Nickel, Copper, Ruthenium, Rhodium, Palladium, Silver, Osmium, Iridium, Platinum, Gold and Mercury.

The New Energy Alchemists (although I don't believe they know they are) collect ORMUS in concentrate from nature's hiding places in water, soil and air by a variety of extraction processes using lye at the core of every process of the transformation. The tight spaces that ORMUS hide out in are the icosahedral shaped molecules in water, salt, air, rock and organic source materials and crystalline sugar due to the Meissner effect... as a superconductor they are able to retreat or be excluded from magnetic fields.

ORMUS is abundant in volcanic soil, seawater, spring water... from all the depths of the earth and in the air, including cosmic stardust.

During much research and studies the New Energy Alchemists reported that ORMUS...

- *Enhances energy flow in the microtubules inside living cells and work to repair damaged DNA.*
- *Assists in the communication between the cells in the body and between body, mind and spirit.*
- *Raises consciousness and vibrancy through nourishing the light body affecting a person, spiritually, physically and mentally.*

- *Has proven to be extremely beneficial to plants, animals and humans who report many healings, rejuvenating and spiritually enlightening effects.*

Some of ORMUS-rich foods are: Almonds, Aloe Vera, Apricot kernels (of the inner pit), Bee pollen (wild), Bloodroot, Blue-green algae, Carrots (depends on ORMUS content of soil), Chamae Rose, Chocolate (organic), Coconut water (wild), Flax oil, Garlic, Goji berries, Grape seeds, Honey (wild), Larch bark, Medicinal mushrooms, Mustard (brown and stone-ground), Noni fruit, Propolis, Royal jelly, Sheep sorrel, Slippery elm bark, St John's Wort, Vanilla, Watercress, White pine bark, Seaweed, Hemp… and many more continue to be tested.

I can feel my heart beating with so much joy, IAM reading yet another source informing me that ORMUS is woven into the fabric of all living things and is the cause for everything to live. Something inside me knows that with each breath ORMUS replenishes and balances my Body Consciousness.

ORMUS is spirit incarnate… Consciousness itself… IAM ORMUS and spirit incarnate… IAM consciousness… IAM All that IAM.

I feel such wonder as life's synchronicity gives me this new information. It all resonates with me and I can feel my consciousness expand with the complete knowing of how energy and life all truly work. My Ormus, the Elemental being is a wondrous bridge between the ancient work of Alchemy Masters and the world of New Potential.

The secret and hidden wonders of the past, is only a small slice of what is going to be possible to bring into my present reality. I know IAM standing on the edge of major new discoveries… *Free Energy* that will power the world is going to be the front-runner, *'but how can we bring this into the world without totally destroying our economics?'* I trust that my consciousness will some how connect with inventive DivineHuman minds through the airways, who will nurture this new seed of creation and allow it to grow in a most magical way.

Like the other elementals I perceived, Ormus is a part of me, a potential I have created to help me awaken and integrate on my journey and expand into a greater awareness of myself. He helps me understand the knowledge of energy dynamics and the transmutation of energy. He has come to unveil the Grand Master Creator within me, and everyone who is listening; preparing Humankind for the biggest show and celebration ever to take place on Earth.

But first things first… he wants me to remember the very beginning of my Divine existence…

Long ago there was only a big space of *All That Is* until one day, I decide I want to have the experience of seeing and knowing myself, to explore and discover my own consciousness and identity, in answer to my question of *'Who AM I'*. So I separate myself from *All That Is*, pure consciousness or spirit.

My separation or at least the illusion of the separation created two aspects: the duality of the female and male (the light and dark, inward and outward) and an intense energy made up of my passion and desire to one day return home, have a process of fusion take place within me and be once again whole and hopefully a lot wiser.

It wasn't until the early sixties when Humankind, one heart at a time, first began to stray away from the flock, from mass consciousness and dare venture out and explore and experience life according to our own individual passion and desire. We had begun to question our role in life and the old ways of doing things. It wasn't long before we realise that each experience is unique and our body responds with a new excitement as new perceptions and insights are gained.

These are ah-ha moments, when the penny drops and our consciousness expands and a process of fusion takes place within Self and Spirit begins to return home. Duality no longer exists, as opposites don't come back together after they have served their purpose and instead evaporate back into neutral energy. This is the moment of oneness, of wholeness… the time Spirit integrates back to Self and becomes One Body Consciousness.

It is the moment New Consciousness is created and Spirit no longer exists as it once did, Spirit is now so much wiser and we become both Divine and Human and a whole new ball game is ready to be played.

Like a contagious dis-ease, new experiences, perceptions and insights create an abundance of New Consciousness, which in turn attract an abundance of New Energy into the physical reality. New Energy of pure love and light that waits patiently in a neutral state to be invited in by each Master Creator, to create new potential and new solutions. A new understanding of love, unity and peace was slowly beginning to permeate the Earth and all Humankind.

A great shift in consciousness, a time of great change is now upon Humankind. We are realising that our old ways of working with the Old Energy Consciousness; attracting energy into life and creating reality and healing and fixing one another is a mental and emotional creation that no longer works and is becoming obsolete.

The New Energy Consciousness is now in play and we can create reality and manifest from our Soul's passion and desire to: know self, express self, come back to self and evolve self into a consciousness and reality unknown to Self, up until that moment.

New discoveries and experiences, beyond anything known or experienced are now here for us to create in our own unique way. There are no books to read, no spirits or ascended grand masters to ask the way. It is up to us to come into action and lead the way.

The orchestration of life is being handed over to each Master Creator… to explore our heart and soul's desire beyond the physical reality and *All That Is Known*. A wonderful time and opportunity to imagine, experience, play and act in joy, happiness and lots of laughter… creating for ourselves a world of love, harmony and unity that everyone has always dreamed about.

Ormus is here to make sure IAM prepared.

As my awareness expands, Ormus takes on a more Human form. He is showing me that he is indeed the potential, the DivineHumanBeing incarnate. He is the integration of Spirit, Human, ALIEN and Earth Authentic Powers... coming together as One Body Consciousness. Ormus is a crystalline self-contained energy being, who uses energy to sustain self. Showing me Humankind's potential to go to the next level... not to cure disease or have better technology, but *to raise Self to our natural high vibration.*

My Body Consciousness is on fire with new excitement and I feel myself expand again. It is necessary for me to stay calm and balanced and put everything into perspective and allow everything to resonate with my heart and soul. Ormus inspires me to write and draw illustrations for an expanded journey with him. The ORMUS Connection...

To help myself first and others if they choose; to prepare to play Humankind's new role as Alchemist, Integrator and Master Creator. It is about awakening to our own magnificence, bringing in and integrating our Divine and Earthly energies in quiet me-time... consciously breathing, grounding, centering and connecting to all our energies above, within and below.

Ormus explains how important it is for all Humankind to awaken to this new awareness and realise the truth of our own Enlightened Divinity and Alchemist self. It is time for Embodied Enlightenment; Ascended Master Creators from all across the world, from each community, region and culture, to walk together and anchor the New Energy Consciousness, co-creating a most peaceful and harmonious New Earth.

The ORMUS Connection...
Awakening to your Magnificent Self...

...Breathing...

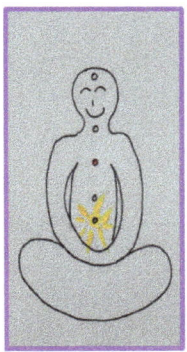

...Connecting...

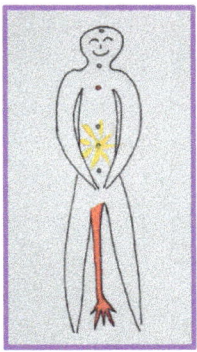

Find yourself a quiet place where you won't be disturbed... Sit or lie comfortably and close your eyes...

Bring your awareness into the NOW moment and focus on breathing calmly and deeply...

Breathing In and Out...
Feel your tummy pushing out on the in breath and relaxing on the out breath... Allow your Body Consciousness (body, mind & spirit) to completely relax...

Breathing In and Out...
Be aware of the aliveness flowing through your physical body and sense the silent vibrant energy bubbling up from deep within your core...

Breathing In and Out...
Allow yourself to fall into your silence, your nothingness... Observe how you feel and what thoughts come up... allow everything to be... no judgement, just relax...

Breathing In and Out...
Know that you are choosing LIFE... choosing to say YES to live your life as you choose...

Breathing In and Out...
Shifting your attention, feel the Earth Energy rising up from Mother Earth... up through your body... through your feet and your invisible tail...

Breathing In and Out...
Feel your invisible tail, feel the energy vibrating inside and outside of it... this is your infinite connection to earth, supporting and grounding you wherever you are...

Breathing In and Out...
Feel the space beneath you, allow yourself to feel safe and unconditionally loved... Own this space beneath you wherever you stand... Allow yourself to feel confident, walk with your head held high and be thankful for being alive...

...Loving Self...

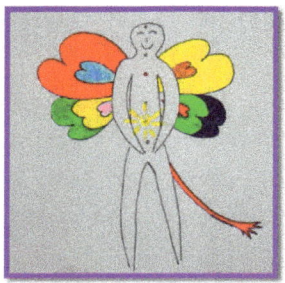

Breathing In and Out...
Know that you are choosing to be inspired... choosing to be the creator of your destiny...

Breathing In and Out...
Shifting your attention to your heart... breathe into your heart, from the front to the back, from the back to the front... Allow your heart to open and expand...

Breathing In and Out...
Feel into your two energy centres, just above the back of your heart... Imagine two beautiful colourful & invisible wings attached here... overflowing with the fullness of your LOVE & PASSION... that emanates out into the world... reflecting the Magnificence that you are...

Breathing In and Out...
Breathe in the Universal Energy, the air that surrounds you... imagine billions of minuscule atoms of light, of pure love... flowing through your body with each breath... integrating with the Earth Energy and your own New Energy that bubbles up from the depth of your core...

Breathing In and Out...
Imagine each cell in your body dancing & vibrating, opening up and expanding into one body consciousness... rebalancing and becoming transparent, open & free...

...Sharing...

Breathing In and Out...
Calmly and Deeply... Receiving and Giving LOVE in the form of a bright colourful figure of 8... Feel connected with ALL that is... ONE vibrating rhythm of life... Connected to the Universe, Earth and your own New Energy as One Body Consciousness...

Breathing In... Receiving unconditional love and support from the depth of Mother Earth to the depth of your core... and Giving your unique love and passion from the depth of your core up into the Universe...

Breathe Out... Receiving love and wisdom back from the Universe, down into the depth of your core... and Giving your unique love and passion from the depth of your core down into Mother Earth...

Know that you are naturally awakening to your IAM DivineHuman Presence... IAM Magnificent... IAM

Me, My Magnificent Self

I felt the presence of Ormus, he was urging me to open up to the ancient Art of Alchemy… he said *'with practice alchemy would become quite natural once again'*.

Alchemy is the transformation and re-arrangement of energy. It is our inherent ability to manifest energy into any form we choose. We are made up of consciousness, not energy. Consciousness when inspired by our passion and hearts desire attracts energy that constantly moves and manifests in temporary states to itself, in order to play and create. After a long period of neglect, the practice of manifestation became painfully slow and unfortunately very mental. When we no longer saw results, we became frustrated and declared that we could do nothing about it. Until the time it became necessary for us to awaken to the truth that we could indeed alchemise quite easily.

It was our Egyptian ancestors that wanted to change the lower vibrations of pain and fear that were on Earth to a new higher vibration that naturally existed in the heavens and within the Earth… and the Art of Alchemy was born. With the energetic density on Earth it was hard to detect or feel our natural high vibration, so they created a portal or vortex for the higher energies to be felt.

They used Pyramids as tools to achieve this and it worked very well, although it didn't work outside the Pyramid. For many years alchemy continued, but just after the time of Jesus, some people (who actually understood what they were doing, put a stop to it, calling the practice witchcraft). This forced the Alchemists to go into hiding. They created laboratories and brought in the metals to act as a smoke screen, telling people that they were transmuting lower metals into higher metals; transmuting lead into gold and stone into precious jewels.

Everyone has the potential to be a New Energy Alchemist, but first it is important to understand the principles of Alchemy...

Riches are not the goal… Alchemy begins within, not on the outside with guides, angels or crystals as this only shuts down our own Chemia...

No force or power can to be used as this only reinforces the object... It isn't necessary to believe, only to know that we can do it and trust creation to do the rest.

Adamus of the Crimson Circle channelled a great inner journey into Chemia that I practiced and experienced many times, and write about here... Please go to the Crimson Circle website (www.crimsoncircle.com) to download for free this journey and experience it for yourself.

An Expanded Journey into Alchemy

I place one of my crystal rocks in the palms of my hands and lie down comfortably with my eyes closed... gently breathing in and out of it... Allowing myself to 'be one' with the rock... accepting it as it is in this moment... Imagining the trillions of atoms of energy that it is made up of... floating in the space of the rock... It has been a rock for many eons but it also has the potential to be anything... I allow myself to expand my perception of what it could be... water... a tree... fire or absolutely nothing.

I see and feel an explosion of atoms... the energy dynamics change as the rock releases itself from the role of being a rock... and now the crystallised energy just floats in a pool of nothingness... I allow myself to expand into this nothingness... breathing into the space and feeling into the crystallised energy that continues to sparkle within the nothingness... I feel overwhelmed with what is happening... The more I breathe into the nothingness the deeper I feel I AM in it... an infinite depth with brilliant whirling colours that I know everything indeed is... everything that I AM too... Master Creator... attracting my hearts desire into my physical reality.

As a Master Creator I imagine the energy of the rock serving me... I visualise the crystallised energies coming together and magically weaving my grand desire into existence.... I breathe into my desire... my creation and allow it to float away in total freedom... I have alchemised... When I open my eyes... the rock is still a rock... but out there... in a different realm... I know my creation has been born and is making its way to me... in the most appropriate way... at the most perfect time.

Ormus is helping me fully integrate as one Body Consciousness, bringing *All of myself* back together as one whole. My whole body and mind has begun to feel much lighter as I know my molecules are naturally taking on a new crystalline structure and I feel myself blossoming with a new radiance. It is time to have some good earned playtime.

Time off to do nothing, rest a lot and maybe a little creating. Tom and myself head overseas for some winter sunshine, visiting our family. It doesn't take long before IAM painting some interesting characters again with my grandchildren Alexander and Milana. A funny mushroom shaped Elemental comes to play with us. His name is Danny and he has a very clear message for me. It's playtime.

Danny… Play-Time and Balancing the Body Consciousness

"Play Time is…
Time for Self to feel life's harmony through play, song and dance that re-balances my Body Consciousness."

IAM not quite sure why, but I find myself spending a lot of time observing and feeling the natural rhythms of nature's harmonious order that pulsate throughout all life. The rise and fall of the sun, the cycles of the moon, the ebb and flow of ocean waves and both my breath and heartbeat are all a constant reminder of life's rhythm pulsating through me.

Life is showing me it is constantly moving, changing and beating as one whole… nature, animals and mankind. The slow movement of the life and death of all things on Earth seem to give ample time for a person to connect with the rhythm and cycle of life and be in harmony. A person's body rhythm that governs the sleeping and waking pattern, determines how much energy one has and influences sociability and feelings. When a person is no longer aware of nature's rhythm and the harmonious affect it has, the body becomes disconnected and lives in a continued state of pressure, chaos and fear. This plays havoc with the body's internal clock, causing it to go into an irregular state of being and the dis-functioning and dis-ease of the body.

IAM putting final touches on Danny's portrait when I clearly understand that it is time for me to get back in touch with the natural harmony of life and what better way than to play, create and act out my heart's desire. Yes indeed it is playtime…. time to express *All of myself* in every way and allow myself to enjoy it all.

Just being around my grandchildren, playing, creating, acting, dancing, singing, sitting quietly and being in nature, helps connect me back to the innocence of living in the now moment… with no thoughts, judgment or labelling. I know this is the beginning of one long amazing and magical adventure. IAM allowing myself to be a unique art form… acting childlike, being real and even foolish, which gives me a feeling of pure excitement and a deep belonging to life.

This new playfulness, being fully immersed in my experience

allows me to see life's beauty and simplicity and be free and limitless. I feel the release of my stuck voice energy and the subtle movement of my loving Divine expression flowing through me. I feel everything is allowed and anything possible… of course, for the greater good of Self and *All of Life*.

I have chosen to live my life in a higher vibration of awareness, consciously choosing in each moment how I want to live my life. I can act and be the Grand Master Creator I truly AM, but I can also consciously act and play out the different Human roles and games that continue to come across my path.

Now IAM with my grandchildren and all I want to be is outrageous, scream out loud and laugh from the depths of my being. The children love screaming out in the park or by the seashore with me and give a mischievous grin of delight when we stop screaming… as if to say… *'Grandma this is great, can we do it again'*… I smile from ear to ear and feel the innocence and joy of us all… and we begin to scream even louder… expressing our voice, feeling magnificent and radiating it out into the world.

IAM in harmony with the natural order of life and this brings me in contact with my deep sensual and sexual self. I feel life vibrating through my Body Consciousness and I experience a deep sense of joy. My Spirit feels renewed, rebalanced and I feel inspired to create great things. IAM indeed dancing to the rhythm of life and feel the love affair between my Human and Divine selves deepening within.

Living life in the confines of the physical reality had stripped my sensuality and sexuality away. Like so many women, during my teenage years of exploring who IAM, I had either been preyed upon or shouted at in disgrace for my sense of dress or my words and actions. Humankind is so deeply obsessed with sin, evil and control over the weaker sex, that the freedom of feeling, being and connecting with the natural world has long since disappeared. Looking back I can see how society, by discouraging our natural sensual and sexual behaviour, has created the problem of sexual abuse, rape, the need for prostitution and insecure, fearful and victimised people.

IAM thankful for all my Human experience, but it is time to move on. It is time to claim and own my sensuality and sexuality, the foundation of the expression of who IAM and the doorway to my innate passion and life force energy of my Master Creator self.

As I claim my own Sovereign and Sacred self... a knowingness comes over me of the suppression of the feminine power and of the need for Humankind to experience domination and control... until the time each person, male and female discovers their own passion and Divine 'power of creation' within themself and no longer needs to be part of the Human game of duality and feed on each others energy for power and accumulation of possessions.

Suddenly my body feels tense and my mind numb... covering up my normal sparkle of joy. I need some quiet me-time... so I take myself off to a place where I won't be disturbed and relax into this dark feeling that has come over me.

Relaxing into my Dark Feeling

Relaxing... breathing... deeply breathing... allowing myself to feel all of my physical body... breathing in and out of each part of me... my toes, ankles, calves, thighs, pelvis, tummy, chest, shoulders, arms, hands, neck and head... relaxing and consciously breathing in my own energy... filling each cell of my body completely with my breath, my energy... and allowing each cell to open up and be transparent...

I ask myself what this feeling is about and in an instant I see a pattern in my body light up... a dark jagged network that stretches and penetrates deeply into all my bodies (physical, mental, emotional and spiritual)... I ask myself what this network represents... and clearly understand how Humankind feed off each other and keep each other in bondage, through all the generations until today...

Codes of programming have penetrated deep into the molecules of Humankind... IAM quite shocked at this insight and ask myself how I can change my programming... override and release them and make new codes for myself...

I breathe deeply in and out of this dark network… It has served me well and through this programming I have learned what I don't like and don't want in my life… With this new awareness I can simply choose to be free of the programming and be my own authentic and powerful Self… I see the network begin to flicker… and feel the need to embrace the programmed network with gratitude and compassion, before the energy releases its hold on me and returns back to where it came from…

Breathing in… Breathing out… Allowing the natural exchange of energies to take place. I spend some time bringing back all my own programming codes that I have given to others… and see them returning as sparkles of light and potential… fusing with my open and transparent cells… filling empty spaces… and my Body Consciousness begins to vibrate in a deep sense of joy.

I remain quietly breathing for a while, enjoying the vibrant feeling of joy. I know IAM no longer in the pattern of bondage with people living now or from my ancestors. I feel light and free.

IAM making it part of my new life style to live more in the present moment, enjoying real things that resonate with my heart. I change what I don't like and allow myself to be adventurous and explore both the known and unknown parts of life. In quiet moments, I hear the pulse of my own heart and soul and feel the urgency of my dream. The dream of my Human heart and Divine soul… to be one within my physical body and mind, being together and becoming aware of knowing Self, expressing Self, exploring the unknown and living in complete freedom.

I know IAM responsible for how I feel in each moment, for my word and action and for creating my own life and destiny. IAM no longer dependent on anything outside of myself or afraid to own my expression. A new voice of confidence is rising; it is my Divine self, allowing me to be wild, free, innocent and magical and be the adventure that I so desire to experience.

Danny hides a lot under his Mexican mushroom hat. I know he is resting after his playtime, mindfully contemplating his experience and distilling the wisdom. I take heed that everything is about balance.

Axiel, who was born at the same time as Danny, had begun to flutter in the corners of my eyes. He has bright coloured wings that span out wide and he flies around me in circles, trying to get my attention. It is nearly time to return home to Spain and say 'see you again soon' to my family in America and begin a new adventure. One play-time is over, it is time to distil my wisdom, to trust my innate knowing and move further; beyond All that is *known* on my journey.

Axiel... Allowing Self a Wider and Wiser Perspective

**"A Wider and Wiser Perspective is...
To expand beyond All that is known and into a
field of All Knowingness."**

As I choose to put my playtime on hold for a while, Axiel the owl I painted in America finally manages to get my attention. I feel his powerful presence around me, mostly during the warm evenings when I sit outside looking at the stars, wondering where my next adventure will take me. When he's not flying around me, he comes and sits near me, high up in my date palm tree observing the evening sky. I feel him breathing calmly and deeply, making me feel at peace and safe. He moves his head and hoots some magical sounds that expand out through the night.

One evening when IAM sitting quietly observing the night sky, I feel my Body Consciousness expand and I begin to perceive the world as if IAM looking out of Axiel's eyes. I see bright lights shimmering in the dark night and notes and tones dancing in the air from every living creature... it is indescribable... but the truth I feel is clear.

The owl is the embodiment of innate wisdom, the keeper of All Knowingness in creation from the beginning of life, gliding elegantly and silently in between the dimensions. He is detached but ever loving and sees connections, relationships and consequences between everything. His love and compassion is the natural consequence of truly seeing and ensures the balance between the light and the dark, the living and the dead, the known and the unknown, underworld and the heavens, keeping everything together and whole.

Axiel wants me to understand that it is now time for Humankind to take over his role and expand out of the limited and fearful mind (identity) that controls our life and into the field of All Knowingness. A field beyond the mind, beyond thinking and figuring things out and just knowing that everything we need to know is available in each moment. This is living as a multi-sensual DivineHumanBeing, a Master Creator self. Living as an inspiration, creative visionary and example of love, peace and reverence for others to resonate with and realise their own truth.

We have had a long Human experience, exploring self and the physical world with our five sensors, discovering what we like, what makes us happy and laugh and what we don't like, what makes us sad and insecure. We have discovered the world of external power and how to control the Environment with physical dominance and competition between each other, in relationships, work and social life. A world of competition where someone's gain is always someone else's loss and breeds fear. Money became the symbol for external power and shaped our economics, creating more and more divisions of the haves and the have nots. We discovered it is not the answer to happiness and security, but the answer to escalating violence, dominance and the destruction of our world.

One heart at a time, through individual experience, our five sensory awareness expands beyond our physical body and personality and we begin to feel the stir of an inner power... An authentic power rooted deep within, a power of reverence that loves life passionately in every form and appearance without judgment and honours everything in each small detail. We remember how to communicate with ourselves, asking questions and listening to answers through our intuition and inner knowingness. We are expanding into the truth of who we truly are, multi-sensual DivineHumanBeings.

I have the need to understand the meaning of the word Reverence; I had heard preachers talk about it when I was younger, but it had never resonated with me. Axiel asked me to relax and consciously breathe and expand into the knowingness of the word. My Body Consciousness began to fill with a flow of information about it...

The downfall of Humankind had begun because of our lack of reverence. We had continued to mimic the Animal Kingdom in its killing and feeding tactics, believing that it was nature's way for the weaker forms of life to exist only to nourish the strong. In our every day life we would curse, judge and use others for our own advancement and success in life. We became arrogant, satisfying only our own needs; polluting the Earth and treading on everything and everyone that was in our way. We were not being responsible for our words and actions and were of the opinion that after we died, it wouldn't matter anyway.

Reverence is about feeling into the essence of each life form, feeling into the true consciousness that everything is made of. Seeing the outer layer, but also the authentic beauty and power that emanates from the core and out into the world. Reverence is to truly honour the unfolding of each unique story of nature, of the Earth and all her inhabitants. Reverence is an attitude of accepting all life as it is and perceiving our reflection in the natural breathing and expanding soul and consciousness of Mother Earth.

As we journey through our life and experience, we can acquire a sense of reverence, developing a capacity to look more deeply at the value of life before we respond in our action. When we recognise our part in creation, the interconnection and interdependency and Divine dance, we have reverence and cannot harm life. We feel safe in the arms of Mother Earth and honour her natural cycles of life and each person's journey toward authentic empowerment.

In a climate of reverence we can align and integrate with our own Human heart and Divine soul and move on from the challenges of the five-sensory world of limitation, brutality and external power, to experience our own multi-sensual authentic power and our heart and soul's desire to live in a new energy consciousness as a Master Creator each person truly is.

Axiel guides me well… IAM expanding with ease and grace into my own true knowingness, the knowingness of my IAM presence that my Human and Divine self is a part of and I now allow to guide me. I trust that answers to my questions come at the most appropriate time, trust to find myself in the most perfect place and able to respond to life in the most perfect way in each moment.

Before Axiel flies off with Jake to other realms, to help regroup and bring home remaining parts of me from other dimensions. He wants me to ponder on the words *I Exist...* words that Adamus had talked about in the Crimson Circle Shouds... and take a last journey with me into my own knowingness.

Axiel assured me that it is important to remember, that no matter what circumstance I find myself in, whether a joyous or sad moment, I can take a conscious breath and be aware of *I Exist.* Nothing else really matters and if I allow myself to just feel into my existence, I will feel my inner passion and potential of *All that IAM* and know that I will attract my own abundant supply of crystalline energy to come in and serve my heart and soul's desire.

My Master Creator self and IAM presence lives in complete harmony with my New Energy that responds to my passion in either a good way or not a good way... it doesn't care, it only wants to serve me. In this way I will always have to be careful with my words... as I receive it all.

An Expanded Journey into my Knowingness
I lie in a comfortable space, relaxing, breathing deeply and calmly, relaxing into myself... Asking myself why I had forgotten not to know... I expand into my knowingness... breathing into it... feeling the gift that I know is innate within and without of me. It is time for me to receive my knowingness fully into my Body Consciousness... breathing into it...allowing my Body Consciousness to receive and expand with the limitless flow of All Knowingness...

I feel my physical body and mind relax.... there is nothing more to learn, nor struggle or doubt, fight another battle or rely on another... Relaxing... Breathing... Allowing...

I know my physical body and mind has intelligence of its own... hidden under all the stress and programming of my long Human experience... but with total acceptance for what it has become... my mind... having nothing left to fight... becomes quiet... and expands beyond itself... into the waters of my Body Consciousness... integrating with All That IAM... and now... becoming the free flow of knowingness... that it has always been... gently guiding me... My Body Consciousness begins to tingle and glow with a new radiance and joy and the light of my knowingness expands deep within and without of me...

Yes my knowingness has always been here, but now works together in harmony with my Human self... allowing me to be clearer and more aware in mind, body and spirit... my Body Consciousness...

I claim All Knowingness as my own... allowing myself to know everything I will ever need to know... the answers and solutions to all my challenges... the riddles within my dreams... without a fight or negotiation... simply by choosing to know in each moment.

Breathing... Allowing... Receiving the original dream of my Divine and Human selves...

Max... Allowing myself to be truly **FREE**

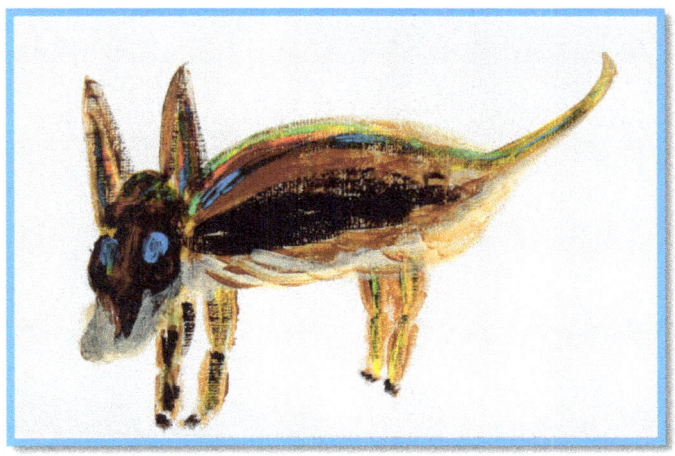

"Freedom is...
To choose to be unlimited and allow myself to expand
into the vastness of my own IAM presence and
experience my heart and soul's desire."

I find myself asking the question *'AM I free'?* Finally free from my Human limited and chaotic mind with its self-destructive thoughts, doubts and appetite for emotional drama? Is this lifetime going to be the last time I play in the duality game, playing the different roles of victim, abuser, rich, poor, healthy or sick?

AM I free from the fear Humankind has created in our pursuit to survive, control and gain power and can I now consciously choose to end my participation in the Human fight? Can I choose instead to allow everything I desire to simply flow into my life and thrive as my unique and authentically powerful Self?

AM I ready to fully let go of my Human biology and ancestral lineage that has served me so well and move forward by myself as one integrated Body Consciousness and play my new role as Master Creator, radiating out a new sense of freedom, love, joy and harmony?

Early one morning as I walk along the seashore I feel someone following me and slowly turn my head and shoulders to find myself looking down into the big brown eyes of a large wolf. My heart makes an extra beat as I take a big gasp of air. *'There is no need to be afraid'*, are words I clearly hear and somehow reassure me that everything is fine and I can take some deep conscious breaths. *'Fear is only an old response to a belief Humankind took on a long time ago, it is time for you to truly resonate and understand fear and release the old belief'.* We are now walking side by side and I feel both calm and excited, looking forward to the beginning of a new adventure.

His name is Max, short for Maximus that describes his magnificent and powerful presence that he indeed radiates. It was Max who had prompted me to ask myself my earlier question… *'AM I free'?* He has come to help me understand the fear that has kept Humankind away from taking the leap of faith into *freedom*. Away from the drama of the limited Human life and expand into the vastness of my own IAM presence, which will allow me to truly experience living in freedom. Or AM I going to continue to live within the constraints of Human misery with people stealing power from each other and pretend that I don't remember Who IAM?

Over the next couple of months I find myself in several situations that show me quite clearly the roles we all continue to play today. As a keen golfer a couple of the situations played out on the local golf course... one with a golfer who was a professional drunk. He was unable to concentrate on his ball, club or target and continuously talked a lot of non-sense and drank alcohol during the entire time we played. The next game I played was with a golfer who thought he was a professional golfer, but with his overly critical focus on his ball, club and target, his grunting and waving hand telling Tom and myself to get out of his way; continued to send his ball everywhere but to the hole on the green. He acted more like a professional loser. Both golfers were very unpleasant and obviously very unhappy in their limited and unbalanced life. I tried hard to focus on my own game, but their behaviour was too unpleasant and at a certain point I had to walk away, otherwise I would have had to act on my urge to slap them both across the face and wake them up from their victim identity.

It seems that everywhere I turn I see someone clearly trapped within their Human identity. *'Do I behave like this too?'* Max is very kind but truthful as he assures me that it doesn't matter. It is all part of the rise and fall of my Human experience, that is ultimately expanding my awareness just enough for me to remember that IAM so much more. It is important for me, however, to understand that just as I have the power to create my experience, I have the power to change it too, simply by choosing to experience something new.

One afternoon, during my quiet me-time, Max takes me on an expanded journey into a most magical and natural place.

An Expanded Journey into Living in Harmony

We are walking slowly through a dense forest of tall fragranced pine trees with striking colours of green. Many paths wind up and down this mountainous forest, the ground laden with a carpet of thick green grass and large rock formations where small animals have made their homes. As we reach the high mountain ridge I can see the crystal turquoise ocean glimmering far below and feel its vibrant beauty.

Natural springs bubble up from the earth and run down in between enormous tree roots that decorate the ground. Max stops to lap up the pure and clear water and I take a closer look at the natural herbs that grow in bushes and lavish displays of colourful wild flowers that fill the air with a wonderful sweet aroma. I can see the details of each flower, the pollen and seeds that are being carried by the insects through the air. Animals go about their daily business, glancing at us as we pass, as if to say hello.

Stone cottages are scattered amongst the rich and wild natural landscape with neatly tended gardens around them. People tended their land and I could smell the delicious home made foods being prepared in the homes. I feel the harmony that life emanates; there is no fear only an abundance of love, joy and peace. Max heads off in the direction of one of the homes, it is simply built from the local natural stone, with open doors and windows... children running in and out of the house laughing as their parents welcome us, inviting us in to sit around the kitchen table and enjoy some chilled spring water and fresh figs off the garden tree.

This loving family explains to me how they go about their day caring, preparing and creating whatever they are innately good and passionate about and this is how they create the harmony I can feel. They live in cooperation and reverence with each other and All of life as everyone has a unique part to play in it.

At the beginning of each day, the families come together for a celebration meal. They take it in turns to prepare and host an abundant buffet of home grown products for everyone to enjoy. Sweet and savoury plants and herbs are grown and wild fish abundant in a nearby sweet/salt lake for the purpose of enjoying tasteful food.

I bring back a feeling of harmony and the sweet aroma of wild flowers and fresh herbs as Max and myself find ourselves back home in the physical reality once again. Max goes on to explain…

Humankind tried to live like this, in harmony with nature and all the Animal Kingdom, but we gradually disconnected ourselves from our true origin. As Human life progressed we became more aware of our own physical mortality and together with the deep inner feeling of lack and incompleteness (having forgotten our origins and where we have come from), we became afraid of our own death.

Fear slowly crept into the very foundation of society and a life of survival was unconsciously created. Domination, competition, greed and power became the normal way to behave.

The strong and powerful preyed on the lives of the weak and unfortunate and it wasn't long before we captured the wild animals, putting them to work, taking away their hunting ground and killing them to eat, sell and gain profit. What was eventually left of the Animal Kingdom took on the reflection of the fear and viciousness of humanity and the animals attacked back. Not understanding what we had created, and out and the need to protect ourselves, we ordered the destruction of all the wild animals. The wolf was one of the many animals that have nearly come close to extinction.

Max wants the truth about the wolf exposed. He is truly a gentle and social creature who reflects his environment, similar to that of Humankind. It was the viciousness of Humankind that the wolf and all wild animals had taken on, not their own. Nevertheless, Max remained hopeful that more and more people continue to remember their true origin and realise the terrible and selfish deeds of both themself and their ancestors and choose to end their individual cycle of destruction and change their destiny to one of living in unity and harmony with All life on Earth.

It is the Human mind… becoming insecure, vulnerable and defensive that has given rise to the fearful and destructive action of society. The mind only knows how to dart backwards and forwards from its past memories and projected future and as the 'unconscious' identification of mind increases, generation after generation, the ego mind with all the trimmings of mental and emotional behaviour begins to take possession and control of its Human self. There is no space in-between our thoughts to consciously breathe, never mind have a quiet moment to sit back, observe and reflect what is happening in our life and be able to stop and change our behaviour.

Humankind continues its selfish behaviour, carrying out its terrible deeds and ways to distract Self from the inner turmoil and fearful mind. We indulge in having more and more food, drinks, drugs, sex, crazy pleasure and dangerous thrills and are addicted to our own ego identity and the continuous search for more. Our addictive behaviour keeps us away from the present moment and feeling the deep inner stirrings of a presence and knowingness within...

The infinite and Divine presence that waits patiently for consciousness to awaken from the identification of form, free itself and expand into a wider field of consciousness of All That Is. A field of consciousness that lies only a breath away, a place where true creativity and beauty is abundant and the natural state of being is love.

I don't play in the game unconsciously anymore, but fear still lingers in my body that is triggered and brings me back into drama. This new understanding of the origin of my fear is helping me release its hold on me.

Max asks me to look back at my childhood, to when some experiences didn't feel quite right or good, but nonetheless, I had lived through them the best I could. He explained that I was no exception and had experienced the negative actions of abuse and disease that are unconsciously passed down generation after generation by our ancestral families for us to repeat or abstain from the pattern of behaviour over and over again, growing in strength... Until each person becomes aware of their own pattern and realises it is not who they are and chooses to respond differently, according to how they feel in each moment.

It is important that I understand that it isn't my true self who has lived all my Human lives, but roles I have chosen to experience during my lives. My Human physical body and personality is only a part of me, IAM so much more. IAM the IAM presence, in soul charge of my Body Consciousness. IAM self-sufficient and create my life and destiny as I desire. I can choose to step out of the Human drama at any given time and forgive myself for all my Human frailty and vulnerability. I can distil the wisdom of all my Human experience and release everything that no longer serves me.

With a new eagerness and greater awareness, IAM ready to commit myself to my Freedom. As my IAM presence, Master Creator self, IAM ready to take my leap of faith into the unknown and live a new adventure in the present moment, beyond time and space with a heart full of joy, a body full of life and a creative mind full of trust and knowingness.

It is time for Max to move on… and his final gift is to accompany me on an expanded journey into my Freedom.

An Expanded Journey into My Freedom…

Relaxing comfortably and consciously breathing… receiving my breath, the breath of life… allowing myself to go deeper and deeper into the core of my being… relaxing… and breathing… being consciously present within my Body Consciousness…

I allow myself to expand into my Freedom… an infinite space of nothingness… only my physical body is floating in the middle of an ever expanding dark space… and then it happens… quite gently… my physical body shatters into a trillion pieces and spans out into the far realms of space…

I know my heart is shattered as I feel it falling away from me in pieces … and now a thousand tears make there way up from the depths… into my throat and eyes… I cry… for a long time… I feel deep sadness… sadness for all the violations, abuse and broken parts of me that has happened throughout All my lives… Breathing deeply… drinking deeply from All of myself…

IAM aware that I have survived it all… IAM here now… aware of a flame deep within my core coming alight… shining… vibrating… and joy flowing through me... I feel as light as a feather... and as transparent as crystal... all my heaviness washes away... deep within... I feel my wholeness... IAM floating in a wonderful space... the darkness has turned into whirls of deep purple/red/pink colours and I know IAM now experiencing everything... IAM an abundance of potential and so much more...

Breathing gently into my light and transparent self... knowing that my Divine self has always been here... hidden under layers and layers of my Human experience... Breathing in and out... and another flood of tears gush through me... but this time they are tears of joy... tears of relief... as my physical Human self realises that I have never been alone... my own Divine light, my IAM presence has been with me... throughout it all... celebrating the joys and comforting the pains... I have never been forsaken. This realisation instigates an almighty explosion within me... nothing could survive... and I see, hurling out into infinite space, energies that no longer serve me.

Breathing calmly... my consciousness expands... and I open up like a lotus flower... I begin to experience receiving millions of tiny crystal atoms of light... coming from outside and from within me... flowing through me... filling me... It is my crystalline Divine self... finally... settling within my Human self... It is time for my DivineHuman self to come into physical existence and experience life as I have always dreamed.

It is a grand dream... the dream of my Human and Divine selves... being aware of each other and coming together in a most wonderful way to give birth to something new... All wise and All loving... The crystalline light body and mind of my Divine self... absorbing and fusing with my physical Human body and mind... The distilled essence of my Human experience of love and compassion... fusing with my Divine wisdom and All knowingness...

My light and translucent body allows me to feel the subtle presence of my Divine self and its crystalline light body... forever energised... alive... rejuvenating and beautiful... and its crystalline light mind... forever aware and All Knowing...

Breathing deeply and calmly... Breathing in my wholeness... Breathing in my freedom...

Max guides me back into the present moment, we have journeyed a lot together, but now it is time for me to allow it all to happen in reality. I feel very much part of the physical world but no longer feel afraid of falling into it. I trust my Body Consciousness to deal with life quite wonderfully and with a deep conscious breath, I drink deeply into *All of me*, situations and people who may concern me and know that everything is OK.

Potent… IAM the Genie of the Lamp, full of Potential

"Potential is…
Me, My Magnificent Self, full of Passion and Desire to Create and Experience life as sensationally as I choose."

I have known since I was a young child that this lifetime was going to be very different, but only now did I truly understand to what extent. Since my birth, my Divine self has been preparing to fully unite with my Human self in order to express its pure and infinite crystalline self in the physical form. This is what I have been mentally, emotionally and physically experiencing for many years. The most gentle and ultimate re-union of my Divine light body and mind... playing and dancing energetically with my physical body and mind. My Divine self passionately caressing and absorbing my physical biology with only one thing in mind, to give birth to a complete and new crystalline DivineHumanBeing, the next stage of Humankind.

This is the greatest love affair I could ever imagine... and it is all mine.

I remember as if it was yesterday, playing the role of Genie in a junior school play *Aladdin and his Lamp*. I had to repeat over and over again the words, *'You have three wishes, what is your command Master?'* Looking back, I find it quite appropriate that my acting Genie coincided at the time my Divine self took a back seat from me as a young and growing child, for me to be able to experience life as most Humanly possible. These last words from my Genie within were said in the hope they would awaken my curiosity to one day explore the magic in life and discover the truth of *All that IAM*... Master Creator of everything I desire. Yes IAM the Genie of my own vessel and these words did indeed echo and stir within me throughout my growing years.

I was in my late teenage years when I first felt the stirring of something so deep and whole within me... the sound of a distant lullaby, not rocking me to sleep but encouraging me to wake up. It was a love song so innocent, the yearning of my Divine self, trying to connect with my Human self and my Human self feeling less than whole searching for something more, questioning, exploring, discovering what life was all about and who IAM. A deep sense of adventure and curiosity took me overseas where I met some wonderful people from many different cultures and truths and I eventually settled down in the wonderful country of Holland.

A decade later, with my perception deepening and expanding quite beyond what I had ever thought possible, I began to recognise my own intuition and how to feel life, rather than think about life… and especially how other people thought my life should be lived. My whole mental and emotional way of thinking and behaving changed.

It was a few years later that I physically began to feel the changes of the gentle integration of my light body loving my physical body, my physical body feeling loved and responsive; moving together in an energetic dance of love… my light mind gently embracing and admiring my physical mind, my physical mind ignoring everything… until many experiences and years later, when my physical mind began to tire of the dull and limited life and didn't want to be excluded any longer, but wanted to feel into the truth and be a part of it all.

My mind had begun to realise that the Human drama didn't matter anymore… peoples' jealousy, judgment, competition and conflict, it would all continue… but without me. It was a huge realisation for me and released the pressure of having to fit in, to do my best and be recognised. It was time for *All of me*, my mind especially, to expand and move beyond.

Coming up to the beautiful age of fifty… I began to feel forceful changes happening within my body and mind and I knew the integration of my light and physical bodies had stepped up the intensity and the reunion of my DivineHuman self was nearing completion.

IAM so thankful that I understood what was happening to me, to be able to embrace it all rather than fall into a spiral of fear and depression that I knew many people around me were doing.

Instead, I actually felt excited to know that something... never to have been done before was actually taking place here on the physical plane and within myself. My Divine self, through its integration and fusion with my Human self was coming into its own magnificent radiance here in the now physical moment.

During some critical times... when my physical body was testing me to the limits, I wondered how I would get through them... but I trusted my body to be gentle with me and accepted what was happening but at the same time kept my focus on the integration of my Divine and Human bodies and the ultimate dream of birthing myself anew... forever energised, rejuvenated, beautiful, forever aware and All knowing.

Each morning and evening before getting up or going to sleep, I make time to relax, consciously breathe into the core of myself and feel into my IAM presence and the words I Exist. My mind sometimes battles with not feeling anything... nothing... nada... but I have patience and breathe deeply into the nothingness... knowing that everything will show itself in time or no time. Eventually my Body Consciousness takes me into a wonderful space... of pure passion, warmth and calmness... my physical body vibrates with a comfortable warm brightness and I expand deep within myself... into infinity and *All That Is.*

Breathing in my Crystalline Love Body...
Deeply breathing... feeling the energetic dance of my Divine and Human bodies... feeling the great love affair... the fusion... and the ultimate birth of my new crystalline love body... part human, part divine, All knowing and wise... balancing, absorbing and connecting with the natural web of All life.... receiving through the conscious breath... my IAM presence... my potential... my energies that are ready to serve me in each now moment.

I breathe into all my ancestral ties... Human death trigger... stuck energy... old patterns and out dated thoughts and beliefs... knowing they are all naturally being released... I embrace them all... they have served me well during my Human experience... Now IAM allowing my natural and integrated Body Consciousness to give birth to an upgraded and detoxified DivineHumanBeing...

Breathing deeply into All that I truly AM... Everything is perfectly OK.

During these intense physical, mental and emotional, good and not so good times, I was inspired to write a love song to myself...

A Love Song
From my Divine self to my Human self

Can you feel me? IAM here
stirring from deep within your core
can you hear me... its time
to untie your chains from all your pains...
I feel your raw grief and sadness
feelings of betrayal, being forgotten
and left behind all alone...
You gave it all, nothing left untouched
from your compassionate heart
but it's time to let go and focus on
loving yourself, trusting yourself
accepting it all... distilling it all

IAM here now... you are not alone
never ever forgotten or unloved
they are just dreams falling away
experiences, expanding your wisdom...
Now its time to love your Human self
unconditionally just as I love you
forgiving yourself for all your moves
wanted and unwanted by others...
For caring and sharing with others
that have yet to learn how to feel,
be grateful for the small things
and the touch of your pure love

Let's walk together now
hand in hand, side by side
your feet caressing the Earth
the wind stroking your face...
Your breath bringing in life
the sea falling and folding around you
the sun beaming down her passion
opening you wide open to feel anew...
The moist salt on your lips, bitter sweet
a kiss so grand from the depth of you
where we begin an embodied union
to be whole... to be physically real

IAM here now... feel me, know me
wipe away your tears
I see you only with eyes of compassion
and admiration, accepting all of you
all the lives and loves you've loved and lost
of not being heard or seen for who you are...
Searching hard for recognition, love
and companionship to fill the empty hours
and the deep void within...
for someone to smooth away the jagged edges
of all your past wounds and hurts
IAM here now... IAM here now

Receive me dear sensual and passionate one
IAM the part of you that brought you here
who gave you this gift of experiencing life
feeling the depths of Human love and fear...
The pain, the suffering, the injustice,
the guilt, the shame and regret
the sharing, the caring, the union
the love, the joy and passion...
This Human life continues
there is no end to the trauma and drama
until one decides to receive me
integrate with me and be whole

IAM here now... waiting
for open arms, open heart and mind
an invitation to come and dance with you
to feel your rhythm and physical being
to embrace and unite as one...
Receive me now with each breath you breathe
feel my caress, what response do you give
touching each other, absorbing each other
surrendering, allowing...
Giving birth to a new creation
of all of me and all of you
the DivineHumanBeing

Together we are one Body Consciousness
a crystalline embodiment of awareness
an enlightened Master of Sovereign domain
daring to love our Self so deeply...
Dissolving all yesterdays and ancestral ties
owning Self completely
with eyes of compassion and a heart of joy
expanding into and beyond the physical...
Exploring new horizons never imagined
bringing in new potential for new creations
walking between time and no time
on Earth and in all space

As with my other elementals, I felt the presence of someone gliding elegantly beside me as I went about my day. I perceived bright colours of the rainbow, the twinkling of the grandest jewels and the ultimate duality of light and dark. Potent is a rainbow snake, my final Elemental being to come back and share the wisdom with me regarding... balance, wholeness, the sacred knowledge of the darkness, my potential and to help me celebrate my transformation and rebirth after a long cycle of Human experience.

IAM entering a new cycle, a new beginning... experiencing my DivineHuman self. I cannot put my finger on how it is all going to play out, but I know without a doubt it is going to be quite beyond anything ever imagined or experienced.

Potent asks me to expand my awareness to include her and bathe in the waters of wisdom. Through the radiance of my new crystalline light, all my darkness, hidden, secret and everything ever resisted was being brought into the light to reveal the ultimate truth that I cannot exist or even experience life without the presence of *All of myself.* IAM the light and the darkness too.

During my Human experience, my Divine self, out of the love for my Human self had kept everything I rejected, feared or didn't like safely hidden away in the dark. Now that my participation in the Human game was over, at least unconsciously, my expanded awareness dissolves the illusion and separation of darkness.

Uncovering the seed of love, of my Divine self… that I truly AM.

Life is my stage now… time to act out my grand love story… boldly, wildly and simply with spontaneity, sensuality and beauty. Trusting myself to move in the most sensual and compassionate way, to live my truth, allow *All of myself* to consciously explore, discover, experience and embrace all… in both realities of time, living in linear time with Human pain, sadness, joy and abundance, knowing that everything has its place and living in no-time in the New Energy Consciousness and creating as a Master Creator what comes next, without the need for my humanness to understand or mind about the outcome.

I have always sensed since I was a young adult that I would live to be quite old, really old (in human years) and now it all made sense. I know the integration of my crystalline light body is ending my aging process and perfecting the art of rejuvenation. I have begun to see bright and shiny copper baby hairs growing underneath my grey hair that I know will grow thick, strong and bright.

My skin is taking on a natural glow of olive tones with a soft and smooth velvet texture. I no longer need to use beauty products except for exfoliate powders/salts to remove my dead cells and my bright lipstick and mascara. My bone and muscle density remain stable, my teeth strong and straight, my eyes rebalancing as I begin to see both near and far much clearer. My body feels bionic and energetic and I don't need so much sleep. My eating habits changed from one day to another… my new integrated body, vibrating much higher doesn't have the need to eat so much food especially sugar and carbohydrates. Instead I enjoy small amounts of quality salads, vegetables and organic farmed dairy, meat and fish… and of course a good glass of red wine or champagne.

IAM becoming more and more inspired in my creative pursuits, my voice allows me to express myself more clearly and I give myself an abundant supply of richness: a new luxury home to relax in, a new comfortable car to get around in, beautiful colourful clothes to wear, good quality food and drink and travel to vibrant and luxurious corners of the world to explore and visit friends and family to share our joyous life.

The integration of my crystalline light mind is smoothing away my unnecessary thoughts and doubts. IAM aware of an ever expanding field of pure love around me, a space that feels safe and real and where I know IAM beginning to spend more of my time creating and living on the New Earth.

My life is certainly all happening… or not happening. However it is happening I *allow* myself to accept and enjoy all moments in a compassionate and trusting way. During quiet me-times, a regular part of my life… I listen to Potent as she reminds me of the important things of living as a Master Creator...

- *A Master Creator is clear about what she wants to express, what she wants to create and how she wants to experience life, as she knows life gives her exactly what she desires in each moment.*
- *A Master Creator allows her creation to be born in freedom and able to expand and grow in its own light, allowing it to express its own joy in the Environment.*
- *A Master Creator has an abundance of Potential in her core being where all life springs forth. Before her presence on Earth, she gifted it all to herself to be able to experience the unimaginable delights of passion, grace, love, joy and abundance.*
- *A Master Creator knows that she is Grace, Joy, Love and Passion, a Divine vessel of overflowing fullness… abundance itself.*
- *A Master Creator knows that her desire to experience delightful sensations in the physical reality is promptly manifested from a constant supply of energy that works in harmony with her consciousness.*

Unfortunately most people don't believe in abundance… the abundance of the Earth or themself, but actually everyone and everything is abundant. Potent wanted me to remember the origin of this belief…

Long ago Humankind believed that there was not enough of

everything to go around and this instigated a race and competition to be the first to get somewhere and accumulate and possess whatever could be found. Our possessions and accumulations made us feel good and secure and our belief in lack settled deep into the core of all Humankind.

Through our belief and misperception about there not being enough, we actually created a controlled and fearful society... which gave us the experience of being rich and poor, but ultimately we created The Victim Personality and an abundance of lack.

When each of us, one heart at a time, realises the truth of our mass experience of lack, we can then choose to release the old belief and pattern of victimisation and allow the abundance of whatever we desire for the good of ourselves and everyone, to come into our life.

Everyone is abundant... When we have no job we may have an abundance of time. When we have a physical ailment we may have an abundance of pain. When we have nothing to do we may have an abundance of boredom and impatience. When we are aware of our limited and mundane life we may have an abundance of limitation, drab and drama.

The secret is to have grace and compassion for our self and channel different energy into our life that resonates with our desire to have an abundantly good life. When we allow ourselves to receive the abundance of our dreams, we are able to give to others if we so choose.

Potent asked me to write a list to summarise my potential, to help me live my life as Master Creator... DivineHumanBeing... and Sovereign self.

- *IAM the potential of Pure Love... Love that I recognise IAM and allows me to be ready in each moment to act out my desire in the way I choose.*
- *IAM the potential of I Exist... the pure state of awareness from where everything arises.*

- *I AM the potential of my Divine Crystalline light mind... All creative and knowing... integrated with my physical and rational mind.*

- *I AM the potential of my Divine Crystalline light body... vibrant and energised... integrated with my physical body.*

- *I AM the potential of my Aspects... Past, Present and Future... integrated with me in this now physical reality.*

- *I AM the potential of Multi-Dimensional sensing... beyond the Human mind/body and physical senses here on Earth.*

- *I AM the potential of Abundance... in harmony with a constant supply of energy that manifests my every desire.*

- *I AM the potential of a Grand Master Creator... exploring and discovering life in a loving, joyous and sensual way.*

- *I AM the potential of One Body Consciousness... my past, present and future, my body, mind and spirit, my aspects, Human self and Divine self.*

- *I AM the potential of All Knowingness... knowing that everything is available to me in each now moment.*

My Awakening and Integration is now complete, my New Elemental family too... Nine beings of my potential, integrated as one Body Consciousness. It is time for me to *celebrate* my Magnificent Self and take all my truths into a new adventure... Loving myself first, Trusting myself completely, Accepting and Understanding *All of myself and All of life* and Knowing All in each moment. Expanding All of myself: my passions, desires and potential beyond all imagination into an infinite spiral of experience as my Enlightened self.

I will continue to dissolve everything that no longer serves me... distil all my Human life experiences into wise and passionate essence... absorb all my physical biology into my new crystalline structure... and gracefully attract and bring in appropriate energies to help me live a most magnificent and balanced life here on Earth.

Barbara... In the Beginning

"I knew there was more. A knowingness that gently guided me into a world full of magic."

I had a good and happy childhood with my family in England, my teenage years reflected my strong will and rebelliousness. I felt different and didn't want to settle for an ordinary life, to have a nine to five job and marry the boy down the road. I was the age of seventeen when I felt an inner guidance begin to stir within me and a deep urge to travel, discover and explore unknown territories, meet new people, experience different truths and ways of being and hopefully answer my burning question… *'Who AM I?'*

I began looking for a job abroad in the British Lady magazine and just before my eighteenth birthday I had everything organized. I had packed everything I owned in two suitcases, said goodbye to my family and headed off feeling excited at the prospect of my new adventure. I felt no guilt or regret about leaving my family behind as I was being driven by a deep passion within.

I enjoyed my newfound freedom on my travels; I met many people from different cultures that had different mannerisms and views. Slowly a whole new world opened up to me, especially after arriving in Holland, a country and way of life that was so very different from England. The Dutch were open to new ideas and new ways of being, tolerant of others, friendly, honest, forthright in their expression and seemingly free from old taboos.

The Dutch resonated with my heart, I felt comfortable and ready to settle and unfold. After several years living in Holland, I met two very important men…Tom my husband and Pieter my teacher, who both played instrumental roles on my journey. Helping me create a strong and solid foundation in which to blossom and awaken to my magnificence.

I felt an underlying passion guide my every move where I found myself in just the right place to meet just the right person. I was becoming more aware of how intricately connected All life is, how everything and everyone is a unique vibration of light in this great creation of life and my unique part in it all.

I experienced a great family life with Tom and our two children, caring and loving each other in our home in Amsterdam. We had a big family on all sides and were often together celebrating each other's birthdays and festive holidays. We travelled to beautiful places on holiday and had caring friends to enjoy great times together. We enjoyed our work, playing golf and sharing deep words of wisdom with one another.

During my five years of self-discovery in a group led by Pieter, I realised how important it was to feel with my heart into each moment and understand what I liked and what felt good to me; instead of relying on what other people thought was good or expected of me. My self-awareness was expanding as I discovered more about myself and I began to like myself in my own right. I resonated with his teachings of there being no rules, no ways and no labels necessary to be able to live a grand and magnificent life. There was only my own unique way, which gave me the confidence to be myself and recognize my own importance, uniqueness and extra-ordinariness. This in turn allowed me to open up and trust that there was something more in life... a divine spark of light that was expanding within me and guiding me in my own truth.

Pieter was quite adamant that *life was all about energy* and how we orchestrate life according to our consciousness. We create our life consciously or unconsciously... with awareness or no awareness. We are the centre and creator of our life and with our conscious awareness we can observe the many old patterns and traditions in our life and be able to choose what we want and how we want to live.

On a similar note we can be aware of new patterns in many popular spiritual trends... To be fair some of them teach self-awareness and encourage people to look at themselves, but they remain patterns that keep people in their mind and playing the Human game... learning, processing and developing to be better, quieter and perfect instead of allowing a person to be truly free.

The mind loves nothing more than to keep a person believing Life is complex and difficult and the development of new practices turn essentially simple truths into complex efforts.

It was of importance that we understand that each person is fully developed, perfect and unique just the way we are and we don't need to attend classes or workshops to improve and develop our self... unless we consciously choose to be distracted and entertained with life's practices. Life in its essence is simple and being aware of our qualities, responsibilities and our conscious breath is enough to bring us into a space of truth and enable us to choose freedom for our self.

I began to realise that Human life is all about experiencing love, through all the wonderful sensations, beautiful places and interesting people that I meet on my journey through life. But along the way I pick up energetic layers of Human conflict that aren't mine and need to be released. IAM beginning to understand that IAM part of something much bigger than myself and there is no separation between what is out there and within me. My outer world mirrors my inner world and if I observe myself in relation to others, I solve the question of who I AM.

I began to enjoy walking in nature, feeling and seeing the simplicity and beauty around me and connect with life in a new way. I began to read, write, draw and paint. I changed my work and found new friends who were interested in my newfound awareness. I could no longer just talk about the weather, the mundane reality and drama that continued to happen in people's lives but about my thirst to explore and discover more. I became a little less materialistic and more focused on expanding into a world beyond my mind and everything that was known.

In the beginning of the new millennium when our children were ready to fly the nest and Tom's work was becoming increasingly hectic, we began to plan for his early retirement and move away from the hectic life and dreary weather to a warmer, quieter and more relaxed environment. A couple of years later, Tom and myself were happily settled in Southern Spain, new horizons, calmer waters and lots of peaceful time to indulge in our passions.

We enjoyed the sunny weather and spent a lot of time outdoors; we both helped out in the community, improved our game of golf and explored our new landscape. I held a weekly awareness circle and monthly creative workshops at home, offering a safe and quiet space for myself and awakening friends to come together and have quality me-time.

We shared our awakening and life experiences with each other, pursued our creative and intuitive talents, connected with our Divine self in expanded journeys, felt into the integration of our Divine and Human selves and allowed ourselves to be the extra-ordinary and magnificent people we truly are.

During my quiet me-time, sometimes alone in my garden or together with friends in an expanded journey or creative workshop I began to perceive Elemental Beings. There were nine in total, all aspects of myself, once lost but now new potential who had returned home to serve me. One by one, over seven years they comforted me and guided me into opening up to deeper truths about myself and life on Earth, reminding me of my true magnificence and urging me to live and experience my Mastery and Enlightenment as my Master Creator self.

Quietness was not all we found... in fact both Tom and I experienced a lot of distraction, resistance and confrontation with people and situations around us. It gave us both an opportunity to face our remaining fears and traumas... to discern, embrace and release them.

When Potent appeared, I knew she was the last of my aspects to come and share her wisdom with me. My elemental family was complete, we had been on a magical adventure together discovering my truth... but now it was time to move on and experience a new beginning.

Tom and I moved away from our beautiful home on the Costa

Calida, travelling further down the southern coast of Spain to the Costa del Sol where we found our new sacred and peaceful home by the sea. A year before, I had painted my dream home, which I recognised as we drove by and without any delay we were able to move in. We love our new home and spend wonderful peaceful days pursuing our creative joys... in a truly magical Environment as Master Creators.

Glossary

I have defined the following words according to my truth (which by all means may not be your truth... as each one's truth is unique) but it may help you resonate and understand my journey better.

All That Is
All existence and non existence

An Expanded Journey
Quiet me-time, allowing Self to expand outside and/or within Self, feeling into the space and experiencing what you sense, whatever it maybe

Ascension
To be fully integrated with all your Human selves, your own Divine light and IAM presence, living life in expanded consciousness as the DivineHuman Master Creator each of us truly is

Aspects
Shadow, dark, broken parts of Humankind that have been hidden or discarded during the Human experience

Awakening
To remember who you are... a Divine loving being, who lives from the heart of compassion in each moment

Body Consciousness
The Human Body, Creative and Rational Mind, Divine Spirit, Past, Present and Future, all aspects... All That IAM

Consciousness
Awareness, being aware of your own existence

Crystallisation
The transformation of pure and translucent light into matter

DivineHumanBeing
The integration or coming together of the Human Being with its own Divinity

Embodied Enlightenment
To be fully integrated with all your Human selves, your own Divine light and IAM presence, living life in expanded consciousness in the physical reality as the DivineHuman Master Creator each of us truly is

Expand
To open and extend Self out into the world or within Self

Freedom
A feeling and attitude that is free from the constrains of the Human limited and linear mind and reality

IAM presence
The original word for GOD meaning infinite knowledge, infinite power, infinite presence, infinite goodness and ultimately meaning I AM God too

Integration
The coming together or fusion of all parts of Self... Human aspects, Alien and Divine force

Knowingness
Being aware and fully present and feeling into the source of all experience

Master
A person who is aware of his innate wisdom and honours and respects all of themself and all of life

Master Creator
A person who knows of their own authentic and sovereign power and creates themself and their life, as they desire in each moment

New Earth
A time-less real space in which to live in peace, harmony and unity… on Mother Earth

New Elemental Being
Sacred Nature Beings of etheric substance, aspects of mankind that come and help, when asked, to re-manifest the Divine on Earth

New Energy
A high expansional and creative energy that exists as PURE LOVE

New Energy Consciousness
An expansive consciousness that Humans create out of their own LOVE to live and create their heart and soul's desire

Old Energy
A low vibrational and mental energy experienced on Earth for many lifetimes

Passion
The burning desire of the Human Heart and Divine Soul or Spirit

Potential
Energy that awaits CHOICE to come into existence

Reverence
To feel into the essence of each life form and truly honour the unfolding of each unique story of nature, of the Earth and all her inhabitants

Sacred
A person of reverence and wholeness

Self sustained
Needing no outside support

She/Her
The feminine part of us, whether male or female

Sovereign
A person who has supreme authentic power and authority over themself and their life

Spirit Incarnate
Divine light in Human form

Spirit / Soul
Divine Light

Synchronicity
When two or more events appear to be meaningfully related

Changes and Effects of the Naturally Awakening Earth and the Human Being

The Earth and Humankind are all part of a Natural Shift of Consciousness that is occurring now. Our solar system finds itself surrounded by a higher vibrational energy, a new energy that we have all called forth in our declaration for no more fear, greed and conflict. It is an energy that resonates with love and naturally raises the vibration on Mother Earth and in all who inhabit her... from the low and dense feelings of fear and limitation that we have created here together over many lifetimes, to the high and vibrant feelings of love and joy that is the essence of who we all truly are.

Love is what Humankind has learned to feel here on Earth and has the potential to create DivineHumanBeings... the next stage of Humankind, living in a peaceful and harmonious Environment, both within the physical Earth and other dimensions simultaneously.

This New Energy, of intense light actually affects the magnetic make-up of the whole solar system, creating intense magnetic storms on the sun, where strong solar flares reach the Earth's orbit and interfere with the magnetics within the Earth and each Human Being. The Human body contains millions of tiny magnetic particles that interconnect through Human antennas to the Earth's magnetic field, enabling the Human to receive and transmit consciousness, which influence the physical body and all of its internal systems.

The interference of the magnetic field causes a cleansing effect, physically shifting and shaking the Earth and her inhabitants, creating unusual weather patterns and within the Human Being cleansing them from all their fears and yesterdays.

It is actually the most beautiful gift that we can receive...

intense light to naturally awaken our consciousness, changing our DNA and crystallising our molecules. Our inner light body is being ignited anew, clearing our body of past debris, burning away everything that no longer serves us, leaving nothing but pure love and passion within each Human Being and the Earth. We are preparing for our re-birth. The DivineHumanBeing, Enlightened and Embodied Master Creators we all truly are.

During this natural shift in consciousness, our awakening is affecting our mental, emotional and physical bodies, pulling us all ways and putting us through some uncomfortable and painful times. Not only are we integrating and releasing all our own past life patterns and karma that no longer serve us, but that of all our ancestors that have lived before us.

Our Body Consciousness, body, mind and spirit is rebalancing and giving birth to a pure new crystalline DivineHuman self. It is of the utmost importance that we neither fight nor give in, as there is nothing we can do, but trust, allow and be aware of this natural happening.

IAM Barbara Franken... Divine Human Master Creator Inspiring New Energy Consciousness

Awakening Symptoms

Physical

- *Aches and pains in the joints, especially neck, shoulders and back...*
- *Heat sensations... beyond the menopause, feeling cold, feeling hot...*
- *Feeling dizzy and shaky...*
- *Vertigo...*
- *Ringing in the ears...*
- *Nausea...*
- *Itchy skin, Red patchy skin, especially the face and hair...*
- *Exhaustion and feeling tired, waking up a lot...*
- *Headaches and Migraine...*
- *Stomach aches and Indigestion...*
- *No appetite...*
- *Extremes of diarrhea and constipation...*
- *Eating a lot...*
- *Heart palpitations...*
- *Irregular heartbeats...*

Emotional/Mental

- *Crying...*
- *Deep Sadness...*
- *Confused...*
- *Nervousness...*
- *Passionless...*
- *Mental...*
- *Anxious...*
- *Intense Dreaming...*
- *Loneliness...*
- *Not thinking straight...*
- *Losing words...*
- *Depressed...*

My suggestions for more comfort each day

- *Consciously breathe in the new energy for a few minutes each morning and evening, especially into painful areas and become one with all...*
- *Eat consciously and healthy, enjoy small portions of protein, good fats, a few berries and lots of salad and vegetables...*
- *Extra supplements of magnesium and zinc...*
- *Moderate use of carbohydrates and sugars*
- *Drink plenty of fresh water...*
- *Moderate use of caffeine, coffee, tea and alcohol...*
- *Positive and Loving self talk...*
- *Soaking the body in warm water and essential oils...*
- *Walk in nature or enjoy gentle exercise each day...*
- *Sleep a lot, naps through the day if possible...*
- *Trust that everything is OK, even when doubts try to creep into your mind...*
- *Remember you are not your mind... You are so much more...*

New Energy Consciousness... Master Creator Class

Does your heart resonate with my Journey?

Do you recognise your own Awakening and natural Integration?

Do you feel a burning excitement... loving yourself so much... to be able to consciously choose and experience living your Enlightenment... your Freedom... now?

I created with the help of sacred friends, Five Master Creator Classes, for us to commit and celebrate our own Mastership, Enlightenment and Freedom... living as Master Creators in the New Energy Consciousness.

You too... can take part in our group here in Benalmadena Costa and be together with sacred friends or join our online class from the comfort of your own home and at your own pace.

It is a wonderful opportunity to put your Self on life's stage and take the leading role in *Your Magnificent Self*.

During five acts you will be inspired to express your innate creativity and spirit/soul voice through *play... dance... song... art... expanded journeys... celebration...*

The Five Master Creator Classes

Allow you to consciously choose to expand out of your Human Identity and into *All That You Truly Are.*

Allow you to release all fears, past wounds and hurts, and move into the expanded identity of *IAM… All That Is…*

Allow you to commit to…
- *Loving and trusting all of yourself*
- *Acceptance and Understanding all of life*
- *The Voice of All Knowing*
- *Discovering the Unknown*
- *Celebrating your IAM Presence*

Allow you to be aware and experience the integration of your Divine and Human selves… Experience yourself as a Magnificent, DivineHumanBeing who decides, chooses and determines how you desire to live your life in each moment.

Allow you to choose to live joyfully in the New Energy Consciousness and experience your own Mastery and Enlightenment.

Allow you to choose to be a new standard and example of A New Energy Pioneer and Builder of our New Earth, here on Mother Earth, taking the next step into the unknown and creating your heart and soul's desire.

Inspire you to create a journal and Master Creator testimony as an expression of your own unique experience discovering your freedom and celebrating your commitment to be your Master Creator self.

Throughout the Master Creator Classes, I will guide you in person, by email, Skype or Facetime. For more information/registration, please contact me by email or through my website.

Connect with Barbara

Website...
http://www.memymagnificentself.com

Email...
barbara@memymagnificentself.com

Twitter...
http://twitter.com/sacredhearts

Facebook...
http://facebook.com/memymagnificentself

Biography

IAM a Creative Visionary & Master Creator... both Divine and Human... creating myself and my life as I desire in each moment.

I love to express *All that IAM* through my Art, Photography, Writing and consciously be Me, My Magnificent self. My creative expression allows me to expand beyond my Human challenges and the *goings on* in the world and remain passionate, vibrant and true to myself... inspiring others along the way.

I live with my husband Tom on the beautiful Mediterranean Coast in Benalmadena, Spain and together we enjoy a relaxed and balanced life... walking in nature, exploring beautiful places, meeting interesting people, tasting good foods and wines and travelling across the seas to visit our family and friends.

My Vision

Humankind, one heart at a time realise the truth of their own magnificence as they choose to hear their Divine voice and allow themself to go beyond all that is known and experience a life of celebration, love, joy and freedom.

My Mission

IAM passionate about creating awareness about The Magnificent Consciousness that each person and All life truly is.

I have created Project Magnificent Consciousness, a creative art project, to bring into local schools and after schools to inspire our young children, through fun and playful activity, to explore, question, discover, experience and express themself in the Magnificent world of Consciousness we live in.

My non-profit Spanish *Asociacion Conciencia Magnifica* funds this project from the sale of my books, Master Creator classes and donations received.

Acknowledgements

With great gratitude I acknowledge the ones who continue to inspire me...

Barbara, my Magnificent Self who I always knew was Extra-Ordinary...

Tom, my gorgeous husband, who challenges, inspires, loves and supports me each day...

Barrie, Gillian and Angie, my loving birth family... always there for one another... no matter what...

My beautiful children and grandchildren, whose love keeps my heart open and allows me to be *who I truly AM*...

Ingrid, my Divine sister who is the sweetness and compassion of life itself and always there for me...

Pieter Freeke, my Dutch 'EigenWijs' Teacher who helped me discover my own colours, qualities and responsibilities, for me to be my grandest Self...

Jonette Crowley, a generous and compassionate woman whom I had the pleasure to meet in Amsterdam for a channelling with White Eagle at the beginning of my Journey. She is the founder of the Centre of Creative Consciousness...

Shambra and the Crimson Circle, my Divine family who have inspired me these last 7 years to be my Magnificent Self...

A special thank you to **Adamus** for his delightful, fun and challenging monthly Shouds that have encouraged me to experience and discover new depths of myself. Thank you for my unique experiences that I have written about and are part of my journey to Mastery and Enlightenment. I encourage others to visit the Crimson Circle website to resonate and experience Adamus's monthly Shouds, Merabhs and Dreamwalks for yourself...

Heather Carlini who wrote a beautiful book *How Solar Flares Help YOU to Evolve*, her wonderful and on going research brought me much peace during my intense light body/mind integration...

Barry Carter for his passionate research into ORMUS (or ORME's... Orbitally Rearranged Monatomic Elements)...

Bruce Lipton for his beautiful book *The Biology of Belief*, an understandable account of the Science behind our Divinity that gave me many ah ha moments that expanded my consciousness...

Shirley Maclaine who's book *Out on a Limb* encouraged me to delve deeper into my truth and not mind about being called crazy...